3.15.78

Mysteries, Monsters and
Untold Secrets

Mysteries, Monsters and Untold Secrets

by GEORGE LAYCOCK

DOUBLEDAY & COMPANY, INC.
GARDEN CITY, NEW YORK

Library of Congress Cataloging in Publication Data

Laycock, George.
  Mysteries, monsters and untold secrets.

  SUMMARY: Fifteen curiosities are discussed.
Includes the Loch Ness monster, Bigfoot, the mystery
of Easter Island, Edgar Cayce, and dowsing.
  1. Curiosities and wonders—Juvenile literature.
[1. Curiosities and wonders] I. Title.
AG243.L37   001.9'44
ISBN 0-385-12741-3 Trade
        0-385-12742-1 Prebound
Library of Congress Catalog Card Number 77–76249

Unanswered Questions

From the times of the earliest people the world has been filled with mysteries. Our ancestors could see the sun and the stars. They could see the lightning and hear the thunder but only guess at what these might be and what they might mean. The coming and going of the birds was a mystery. The darkness of night, the frost that killed the plants, the coloring of the autumn leaves went unexplained.

People searched for the answers. What they could not explain was said to be magic, or the will of the gods.

Gradually we have found the answers to many ancient questions. Science can explain the passing of the seasons and the travels of the birds. New information is added constantly to what we know.

But the world is still rich in legends, strange happenings, and unsolved mysteries. Some are natural, others are caused by man, and for many the mysteries grow deeper with the passing of time. These are the great unsolved puzzles we explore in this book.

In time we may know that some of the mysteries exist only in our imaginations, that they are not real at all. Or we may prove they are real. But now, and perhaps for a long time to come, these legends and mysteries are unexplained—and sometimes frightening.

GEORGE LAYCOCK

Contents

CHAPTER I

New Look at Loch Ness

One spring evening I drove to the nearby college town of Oxford, Ohio, to hear the latest news about the search for the Loch Ness monster. I went as a doubter. I never said flatly that there is no such thing as the Loch Ness monster. How can one be that certain? But the probabilities seemed slender.

Those convinced, however, that this famous monster really lives appear to be closing in on it as the years pass. In Scotland, where the Loch Ness monster is fondly called Nessie, there are many who claim to have seen it. Indeed, people have been seeing Nessie off and on for more than fourteen hundred years. Saint Columba is credited with one of the very first sightings, in 565 A.D. Since then the reports have continued until today more than a thousand people claim to have had at least a brief glimpse of the elusive beast.

Nessie makes its home in Loch Ness, a deep, cold lake in northern Scotland. This loch is 23 miles long and in places more than 750 feet deep. The River Ness flows down through the loch on its way out to the sea.

These brown waters are so colored by peat that the human eye can see no more than a few feet through their murky depths. A diver could be very close to one of these monsters without even knowing it. Perhaps this has helped Nessie remain one of the best-hidden monsters of all time.

For many decades people were inclined to take Nessie lightly. Many still do. But such skeptics change their minds fast once they've seen Scotland's favorite monster.

After a new highway was carved on the hillside along the west side of Loch Ness, a growing number of people came to visit the beautiful northern lake. With more people coming, one might expect that the monster sightings would increase. That is exactly what happened. During 1933 and 1934 Nessie was spotted by more than forty people.

Among the more startling reports was that of the MacLennan family. The MacLennans went for a picnic on the beautiful grassy slope above the loch near Urquhart Castle. The children were playing quietly. The scene was a peaceful one. Mrs. MacLennan kicked off her shoes and strolled up a small hill that led down to the water. As she topped the knoll the grass felt cool beneath her feet and the whole world seemed at peace.

Then she looked down the gentle slope to the water's edge and a cold shiver swept over her. There, lying on the bank, was a huge animal, the strangest-looking creature she could imagine. Its great flabby body was a dirty, dark gray color. Its neck was stretched out on the grass and it seemed to be napping. Mrs. MacLennan screamed.

With this the monster raised its head, and when it saw Mrs. MacLennan it heaved itself up and scrambled toward the water. Later, as she recalled the features of the animal, Mrs. MacLennan said that it lifted itself on short stubby forelegs and that its feet were large hooves shaped somewhat like those of a giant pig. Its rear legs dragged. As the creature slid heavily into the water, Mrs. MacLennan's children reached the scene. But they were too late to see anything except the rings of water where the animal had vanished.

Five years later a tugboat captain was steering his boat across Loch Ness. Everything seemed to be in order. The sky was cloudy just as it is much of the time around Loch Ness. The water was rough from the wind. The tug plowed on mile after mile, its engines laboring normally. The captain was not thinking about monsters. He didn't believe in Nessie anyhow. He made this plain enough to anyone who asked him if he'd ever seen the beast. Then, beside the boat, a creature like nothing the captain had ever seen before stuck its long

In this section of Loch Ness, near the ruins of Urquhart Castle, Nessie has been reported many times. (*Photo: British Tourist Authority*)

humped back out of the water. It had a long, slender neck and a little head. The monster rushed ahead, gained speed on the tug, and disappeared far out in front of the boat. This was enough to change the captain's mind. As far as he was concerned, Nessie was real, after all.

Other sightings even included an observation by a driver who saw Nessie in the beam of his headlights on a dark night as the monster crossed the highway near the loch.

These stories were told and retold. Word of Nessie spread around the world. This did a marvelous thing for Scotland. Tourists began to visit Loch Ness, hoping for a glimpse of the elusive lake monster. Tourism can be good for a country's economy. Nessie, real or not, became the most valuable animal in all Scotland.

But the lecturer who was to tell us about the Loch Ness monster that night in Oxford, Ohio, had brought scientific methods to the search for Nessie, and people were eager to hear his message. All the seats were filled and students stood around the walls and sat in the aisles to listen to the story Robert H. Rines had to tell.

Dr. Rines, president of the Boston Academy of Applied Science, led his first scientific expedition to Loch Ness in 1970. He took along modern sonar equipment and used this to "see" into the murky depths. Sonar works by sending high-intensity sound impulses into the water and measuring the echoes sent back as the sound waves bounce off the bottom or off objects between it and the bottom. It can reveal the depth of objects in the water, their size, and whether or not they are moving. That summer the sonar equipment showed the researchers important facts. There were large moving objects in the loch. Also there were abundant fish to feed monsters.

Dr. Rines meanwhile was consulting with his colleagues, searching for still better equipment for gathering information about the monster of Loch Ness. He worked with Dr. Harold E. Edgerton, who, as a professor at Massachusetts Institute of Technology, had pioneered in the development of high-speed underwater photography. Dr. Edgerton had also developed remarkable strobe lights for making pictures in dingy water. Now, he designed a system of lights Dr. Rines might use to obtain closeup pictures in Loch Ness.

Dr. Rines linked his camera to the sonar and set it so that it would begin making pictures automatically as soon as any large object passed through the sonar field. It would continue to make pictures every fifteen seconds as long as the sonar told it to.

For their first test, the crew of monster seekers chose the bay where Nessie had most often been sighted. They carefully cleaned the camera lens, then began lowering it gently toward the lake bottom. Divers checked it there and found it clean and ready to make monster pictures.

Another camera was suspended under the research boat and pointed downward into the dark water. All that was needed now was to wait for Nessie to come nosing about.

But a strange thing happened. The lens of the camera on the bottom of the loch was suddenly covered with sand, apparently kicked onto it by some large frightened creature. Had Nessie been there and kicked up the silt?

That camera, with its sand-covered lens, made no pictures. But the other camera, hanging beneath the boat, was still in working order. It yielded pictures that to some looked plainly like parts of a huge unknown monster swimming in the water. These color pictures were perhaps the best evidence yet that there really is a Nessie. In 1975 Dr. Rines and his crew were back in Scotland with still better photographic equipment, and the pictures they took were among those shown to the audience in Oxford.

One famous picture, believed by some to be Nessie, was made in 1934 by a noted physician who was vacationing on Loch Ness. It showed a large, dark creature swimming on the surface. Its long slender neck and small head stuck out of the water. No one was ever able to prove that this picture had been faked. Neither could anyone suggest a reason why the photographer would want to set up such a hoax. But this picture, like others made later, was rather indistinct. So, for that matter, were those made by Dr. Rines and his crew in 1972 and 1975.

But, sitting in the darkened auditorium, we saw the

This is an official British Government photograph showing what many believe to be part of the Loch Ness monster swimming in Urquhart Bay on Loch Ness. (*Photo: British Tourist Authority*)

head of a monster in murky water as it filled the screen before us. It was lumpy and appeared to have a wide mouth where the mouth should be. It also seemed to have two small horns on the top of the head. But perhaps these were not horns. Some believe that they may, instead, have been breathing tubes. This supports the theory that Nessie is a huge reptile that must come to the surface to breathe.

Another picture revealed a large angular object that could have been a flipper, four to six feet across. It was attached to the side of what might have been the body of Nessie.

But the research team also wanted to know more about the nature of the lake deep below the surface. They hoped to learn whether there really were places where large creatures could hide.

This search was concentrated on Urquhart Bay, where Nessie has been most often reported. On the research vessel *Narwhal* the scientists cruised back and forth over the bay, taking soundings and pictures and transferring the information to a map.

For the first time they began to understand the truth about this arm of Loch Ness. Underwater, along both sides of the bay, were deep hidden ravines, rocky canyons and caves, dark recesses far below the surface. This excited the research team. The hiding places made the whole story of Nessie more believable. Nessie, it was agreed, could cruise about down there among those dark caves without sending a ripple to the surface.

This is also the area in which one earlier investigator heard strange underwater sounds the year before, tapping sounds that no biologist has yet been able to identify.

These are the bits of evidence that help convince a growing number of people that there really is some "large animal" living deep in Loch Ness. Studying the accumulated evidence, Dr. George R. Zug, curator of amphibians and reptiles at the Smithsonian Institution in Washington, D.C., said, "I started as a skeptic. Now I believe there is a population of large animals in the loch. I don't have any idea of what they are." But he is convinced that research should continue and that the mystery of the Loch Ness monster should be solved.

Another scientist calling for more such research is Dr. Alfred W. Crompton, professor of biology at Harvard University. He, too, believes that the evidence points to a large aquatic animal living in Loch Ness.

What kind of animal this might be is little more than a guess. The most frequent speculation is that Nessie is an ancient reptile, a plesiosaur believed extinct for fifty million years or more.

This is not the only such monster reported from deep lakes over the years. For more than half a century people around Montana's Flathead Lake have thought there might be something very large and unidentified living in the depths of that cold lake. Indians told the earliest white people about this monster. The monster of Flathead Lake is said to be at least twenty-five feet

Beneath the misty shadows of Loch Ness, where the water, hundreds of feet deep, hides dark caverns, may be the home of the world's best-known monster. (*Photo: British Tourist Authority*)

long and uniformly black, and to swim on the surface, sometimes creating huge waves even when the rest of the lake is calm.

In 1922 scientists in Argentina were choosing sides on the question of whether there could be a similar monster in Patagonia. An American mining engineer was among those who had sighted such a creature. What he described had the size, outline, and features of the ancient plesiosaurs. But there has been little heard of this population of monsters in recent times, and if they were indeed there, they may by now have become extinct.

The mystery locked in the depths of Loch Ness may be closer to an answer than ever before. Dr. Rines and Sir Peter Scott of England have even given Nessie a proper scientific name, *Nessiteras rhombopteryx,* meaning "Ness marvel with a diamond-shaped fin." Some believe that science will soon solve the ancient mystery.

Meanwhile, officials in Scotland have taken steps to protect Nessie. They warn that their famous monsters, if they are really out there in the cold waters of Loch Ness, must be among the world's most endangered wildlife. Anyone harming, or even teasing, a Loch Ness monster can be arrested.

CHAPTER 2

Strange Lights in the Night

Some of the mysterious lights people see in the night sky can be explained. Reflections of searchlights on strangely formed clouds have startled whole communities. Naturally phosphorescent materials have suddenly appeared in mysterious ways.

But there are other lights, soft glowing forms that drift in the darkness and defy all efforts to explain them. Such lights have been reported since ancient times. They can appear anywhere. With the passing of time, they may become local ghost stories because people can find no other explanation.

Such a light is said to have appeared many years ago over a railroad track in North Carolina near the Virginia border. The engineer and the fireman watched wide-eyed as a light above the tracks came directly toward them. They were going uphill at a slow speed and the engineer stopped his train because he was certain another train was about to crash headlong into them. At the last instant both engineer and fireman leaped from the engine and rolled down the embankment and into the weeds.

When they realized there had been no collision, they climbed back up to their waiting engine. The light was gone. It is said that the fireman was so shaken by the experience, and bruised by his fall, that another workman had to take over his duties and help bring the train into the next station.

This light was seen first in 1867. That was the year Joe Baldwin had his head cut off. Baldwin had climbed down between two cars for what should have been an easy job. He had done this hundreds of times. One of the cars had become uncoupled, which called for a workman to get down between the cars and put the iron pin back into the links connecting the two cars. Baldwin, his lantern in hand, was carrying out this duty. The train lurched and Baldwin was caught between the cars in a freak accident that removed his head.

Within a few weeks the first incidence of the strange light occurred along that section of the railroad. And the reports continued, the light appearing silently, drifting a distance along the tracks, then vanishing without a trace. Dozens of people insisted that they had seen it there on many nights. Some people have since theorized that it was merely the reflection of automobile headlights from a nearby highway. But there was no nearby highway and automobiles had not yet been invented.

Others have said that the light is Joe Baldwin's lantern, and that Joe Baldwin is out searching for his head. When two lights appeared, people said Joe Baldwin had brought along someone to help search.

For a while an investigator, down from Washington, D.C., tried to unravel the mystery of these strange lights. The lights were like nothing he had ever seen before. On occasion the light was seen weaving along about five feet above the tracks, then arcing through the air and vanishing in the weeds. But no search ever revealed a trace of anything.

This ghost light was seen for many years, and the story of it was even repeated for a President of the United States. In 1889, when Grover Cleveland was President, his train once stopped near the very place where Joe Baldwin had lost his head. The President noticed that the brakeman carried not one lantern but two. One was white, the other green. The President asked the brakeman the purpose of the two lanterns. With two lights, of different colors, he was told, engineers would know that this was not Joe Baldwin's light, and therefore would not endanger their trains by obeying any false signals the mystery light gives.

In the mountains where West Virginia, Virginia, and

Kentucky meet, travelers may still hear the tale of the green floating head. The names have been changed to protect the dead. People living in the cabins up Coal Hollow had never thought of locking their doors before they heard about the strange light floating over Hickory Ridge. Hickory Ridge was the highest place in the area and from there you could look out for miles in every direction.

The unexplained light, seen by several dependable witnesses, was about the size of a basketball. It was a pale creamy green, and most of the time it drifted slowly along beneath the trees. It stayed close to the earth, about as high above the ground as a woman's head.

This moving, soft green light did not dodge around trees. This was confirmed one dark night by two brothers running their coon hounds on Hickory Ridge. Suddenly one of the hunters came to a sliding halt and stood stock-still in the dead leaves. His brother, a few feet away, also stopped. They were shivering and both were speechless. Coming toward them was the green head. Later, one said he thought for a moment he could see hollows where two dark eyes stared out of the misty green globe. The other was never sure he had seen the eyes.

But they knew one thing—the light came directly toward them. It did not swerve to miss the trees. Standing between the two hunters was a giant oak tree. One hunter said later, "It must have passed on your side because it disappeared just long enough to get past the tree." His brother swore it passed on the other side of the tree. Then they understood. The light had gone right through the solid wood as if it had not been there at all.

Three nights later the light was seen again. This time a schoolteacher was crossing the mountain about midnight, coming home by the shortcut after spending the evening courting over in the next hollow. By the time the teacher came to Hickory Ridge he could barely see the trail. The sky had clouded up and the woods were filled with the low rumbling of distant thunder. The teacher suddenly felt a chill even though it was a hot summer night. He had heard about the strange light up on Hickory Ridge but he had never believed the story.

Then he glanced up from the trail, and as he lifted his eyes, there, coming directly at him, scarcely ten feet away, was the floating light.

The teacher recalled later that he thought the glowing ball looked cottony, or like a tiny round cloud. Filmy tails flowed out behind it like soft hair. In the front of the glow were two dark hollow places that gave it the look of a ghostly face.

At the final instant the teacher dived into the briars beside the trail and for some minutes lay there too shaken to move. He felt as if his arms and legs had turned to ice. The light disappeared on down the trail, passing through trees and rocks until it vanished over the mountain. Gradually the teacher was able to stand again and work the coldness from his limbs. He had the strange feeling that if the light had touched him he would have frozen to death.

For two days afterward he refused to tell people down in the hollow what caused the scratches the briars had made on his face and hands. But when he finally told of his meeting with the soft green light on Hickory Ridge, nobody argued. Too many had seen it to doubt that it was really there.

Slowly the reports of the moving light on Hickory Ridge died down. Fewer and fewer people saw it. In part, this was due to the fact that people almost never went up on Hickory Ridge at night anymore.

But old-timers gave the strange light a lot of thought. They compared notes. Finally they reached a conclusion that became widely believed up and down the hollow.

Some months before the light was first seen, Sterling Carter returned to the hollow with his new bride. Marcie Carter was a beautiful young woman, perhaps as pretty as any who ever came to those hills. She was immediately popular with her new neighbors.

Then one afternoon when Sterling was out in the woods sawing trees, Sam Campbell stopped by the Carter cabin and was still there talking with Marcie when Sterling came in from the woods. Rumor had it that he didn't like Sam Campbell anyway and especially didn't like his talking with Marcie.

The two men must have argued, then fought. As the scene was reconstructed later, Sterling tried to kill Sam with his squirrel rifle. Marcie leaped to stop him, but she stopped the bullet instead. By this time Sam was upon the young husband, and in minutes Sterling, like his wife, lay dead upon the cabin floor. His body was found there. Marcie Carter's body was found in an old abandoned coal mine nearby. Sam Campbell was never heard of again.

It was in those weeks when Marcie Carter's body lay in the old mine that the floating light first appeared on Hickory Ridge.

Stories of such unexplainable lights, when told and retold, may change from fact to half fact. Or they may begin with a local storyteller's imagination. But ghost stories and imagination do not account for the hundreds of sightings of flying objects that investigators group together and know as UFOs.

CHAPTER 3

Have You Seen the UFOs?

The people who take unidentified flying objects most seriously are those who have seen them. It would, for example, be difficult to convince one policeman in Elmwood, Wisconsin, that there is no such thing as a UFO.

This officer was on duty at eleven o'clock on the evening of April 22, 1976, when he paused to look toward the top of Tuttle Hill. There on the hilltop was a strange glowing light. The officer radioed into headquarters that he was going to investigate.

The dispatcher heard no more from the officer until his patrol car reached the top of Tuttle Hill, and what she heard then was enough to make her shiver. The officer reported that a genuine UFO had landed.

Detail by detail, he started to radio a full description of what he was seeing. Then his radio suddenly went silent. Another patrol car was immediately dispatched. Meanwhile, the officer's wife, who had been monitoring the radio calls at home, also heard her husband's report of the UFO. She hurried to the scene in their family car.

But first to reach the scene was a local citizen who had sensed that the officer was in trouble and stopped to check. The police-car door stood open. The officer, sitting behind the steering wheel, seemed dazed and was not making much sense.

The policeman who reported the UFO sighting spent the next four days in the local hospital, recovering from extreme nervousness. Then he was interviewed by a trained investigator from the Center for UFO Studies. The center, which is a privately run research group in Evanston, Illinois, collects and studies information on new sightings of UFOs from all parts of the world.

"When I got to the top of Tuttle Hill," the officer told the interviewer, "there was this huge object that appeared to be about as high as a two-story house and about two hundred fifty feet across. It was about five hundred feet away and one hundred feet off the ground. There was an orange-white light at the top and six bluish-white lights on the side and I could see shadows as if someone were moving inside it." The officer believed there were legs sticking down from the UFO, and a long black hose projecting from it.

He watched the ship rise into the air at high speed. As the UFO lifted above the hill, a blinding light flashed and in that instant the patrol car's electrical system failed. The lights went out, the radio fell silent, the engine stopped. The officer did not recall anything else until he heard someone asking if he needed help.

No one, including the police officer, knows what he witnessed on top of Tuttle Hill. The officer was the only one to get a really close look at the invading UFO. That same night, however, other people from several parts of Elmwood also reported seeing the strange bright lights.

Less than a month before, another UFO had been reported in Pennsylvania. This one was seen at eight o'clock in the evening by three people, a mother, father, and their young son. The family was riding in the family car at the time. They all agreed that what they witnessed was a round flying object, yellowish, with a row of square panels around its center. The machine came within four car lengths of them. They all saw it rotating and heard a "chirping" sound.

They stopped their car and sat staring in disbelief at the UFO. They tried to remember everything they were seeing. Illuminated legs lowered from the bottom of the UFO. For twenty minutes more they sat there and watched this unbelievable drama. Then the object vanished behind a row of trees. Aside from their memories, the only evidence they had of anything unusual was the way they felt. The child's eyes burned and itched. His mother was dizzy and suffering from nausea.

UFOs are among the greatest unsolved mysteries anywhere. Many people doubt that they exist at all. But, according to one public opinion poll, more than five million people, worldwide, claim to have seen such objects in the sky.

In the last quarter century the UFO sightings have multiplied. There have been so many sightings that the reports cannot be easily ignored. The United States Air Force has carried out major investigations of UFOs.

Today, a number of groups are studying unidentified flying objects in various parts of the world. They are trying to answer the basic questions of what it is that people are seeing out there in the sky, where these flying objects come from, and why they are hovering around the earth.

UFO sightings are not new. They have been reported for centuries. If we are to believe ancient records, those seen by people long ago were much like what people are still reporting. A flying wheel in the sky, bathed in fiery light, was reported in the Old Testament. In 1896, seven years before the Wright brothers flew at Kitty Hawk, whole squadrons of UFOs appeared over California. In November of that year one was sighted over the home of the mayor of San Francisco. Observers said that it hovered overhead, had a row of powerful lights down one side, and flew swiftly and silently when it vanished to the west.

Two weeks later there was a rash of reports from people who had sighted strange lights in the sky over Sacramento. On one evening, practically everyone working for the local streetcar company saw the lights from different parts of town. When they assembled for work the following morning they compared notes and could talk of nothing but the mystery ships.

Around Sacramento, however, there was skepticism. Some doubted that the streetcar drivers had really seen anything. The idea of flying objects was ridiculed in the saloons and laughed at by newspapers.

Then on a Sunday afternoon later that month, a strange series of events occurred. Darkness arrived ahead of schedule that day. By 5:30 P.M. daylight was gone, and the sky was blanketed by threatening black clouds.

The strange light first approached out of the northwest, blinking against the dark clouds and heading straight for the heart of Sacramento.

The first person to see it rubbed his eyes, stared again, then began racing down the street yelling at the top of his lungs. People tumbled from buildings everywhere. Streetcar motormen, plainly seeing what they had tried to tell everyone about for days, raced across town clanging their engine bells loudly and pointing to the sky. For half an hour the object cruised over the center of the city. Thousands of people saw it that evening before it vanished. Even the newspaper reporters who had scoffed at the earlier reports became believers.

Talk of the UFOs, which were not yet known by that name, went on for days.

For several weeks the reports continued from various cities in central California. Typical was a story carried in the *Weekly Delta,* published in Visalia, California. On the evening of November 26 several local citizens had sighted an "airship." It was traveling northwest, said the paper, ". . . at an apparent speed of a train of cars in a straight line; then it moved upward, then downward, then to the right and again to the left. . . . The light was surrounded by a halo, the prismatic beams of which so dazzled the eyes of the beholders that the true form of the ship was obscured."

Later in the month, people in Los Angeles had a glimpse of the remarkable lights that had startled sister communities to the north. They saw two lights at one time speeding across the sky high over Los Angeles.

The UFOs that appeared over California in 1896 were much like others witnessed in recent years. UFO investigator Loren E. Gross, who has studied the California sightings and written about them, believes that the rash of sightings over California in 1896 was the first major wave of UFOs recorded in modern times.

Other reports occasionally filtered in from around the country during the 1920s and 1930s, but never were these sightings as spectacular as those that occurred in California in 1896. Then during World War II and the Korean War, combat pilots began seeing more and more of the strange, unexplainable lights.

Perhaps the most famous recent sighting was near Mount Rainier, in the state of Washington, by private pilot Kenneth Arnold. As a trained pilot, Arnold was able to make some judgments of what he saw.

When he landed, he reported to a newspaperman and to airport employees that he had seen silvery disk-shaped craft darting about over the peak of Mount Rainier at speeds of about seventeen hundred miles per hour. What did they look like? "Like flying saucers." That term caught on, and any strange object sighted in the sky thereafter became a "flying saucer."

While many took the report lightly, the Air Force was becoming increasingly interested. Four days later one of its pilots reported seeing five UFOs passing over Nevada. Other reports followed. W 1996094

Late one night in the 1950s a large naval aircraft was flying a southwestern course toward Newfoundland when a bright yellow light appeared on the sea perhaps thirty-five miles ahead of the plane. The pilot, a man of long experience in transoceanic flights, wondered if he might be seeing a city, ship, or other aircraft. But his navigator soon assured him that there was no land down there, nor were there supposed to be ships or other aircraft in that area.

Time had come to awaken the relief crew, and as the new crew came forward they too could plainly see the circular light. They were now within seven miles of it and it was still apparently at water level.

Then they saw the yellow light go out. An instant later the object was surrounded by a fiery orange-red light instead. "It was moving toward us at a fantastic speed," said the pilot.

The men in the naval plane thought they were going to crash into the onrushing craft. They began ducking for cover while the pilot quickly switched off the autopilot and made ready to put his plane into a sharp dive in order to avoid collision.

Then the unidentified craft stopped in midair. It was as if it had been at water level, seen the plane, and come up to investigate. Now it flew below and to one side of the naval craft, looking like a giant saucer tilted slightly. The pilot thought it looked metallic and might be two hundred to three hundred feet across. All around it there was a purple-red glow.

After flying in this position for a minute or more the object backed off, then without turning, sped away into the sky and quickly vanished. The pilots estimated its speed at more than fifteen hundred miles per hour.

The officers learned two interesting things when they landed. First, there had been several similar sightings recently. In addition, radar operators at the airfield in Newfoundland had seen the object on their screens and tracked it at speeds greater than eighteen hundred miles per hour.

Since then, the number of UFO sightings has increased every year. Books have been written about them. Official investigations continue. A growing number of people take them seriously. Some believe they are coming here from other planets.

Are the strange lights seen in the sky really spaceships

The *Pioneer* spacecraft, designed to give scientists on earth a closeup look at the planet Jupiter. Frequent sightings of UFOs raise the theory that the earth may be under observation by beings from distant planets. (*Photo: National Aeronautics and Space Administration*)

and are there intelligent beings commanding them? Some researchers believe so. David Webb of the Center for UFO Studies said that 1973 brought an especially large number of reports of such beings in relation to the UFOs. In his report, "1973—Year of the Humanoids," Webb said, "I recorded seventy reports of this type during the five months from August through December, 1973." Fifty-five of these were from the United States, with seven of them seen on a single day in October. Most of these occurred in the eastern half of the country, especially in New Hampshire, Ohio, Pennsylvania, West Virginia, North Carolina, Florida, Georgia, and a few other states. California reported three sightings of humanoids.

During this period the humanlike creatures were seen at least three times near Hartford City, Indiana, about halfway between Fort Wayne and Indianapolis. The first person to report them said that there were two of them wearing silver-colored suits. They stood about four feet high and hobbled across the road in the lights of a local woman's car. As she came abreast of them they threw up their arms and made frightening noises.

They were spotted again a short time later, still lingering near the road. The couple who saw them this time had a somewhat better look. There were no features on their silvery faces and their bodies appeared bulky and shapeless. When they moved, they danced about in a manner not characteristic of humans. The couple who saw them remembered the feet because the feet were square. The following day the soft earth was marked with square tracks.

Next the pair of humanoids was seen in a freshly plowed field about seventy-five feet from the highway. The man who saw them this time was driving a pickup truck, and to get a better view he swung his truck around so that the headlights would shine upon the strange creatures. They turned squarely toward him and the glare from their silvery suits blinded him. He quickly turned off his truck lights, but he could still see them plainly. He, too, noticed their square feet. He could also see their heads, which were egg-shaped. Hoses hung from their heads to their chests.

Up to this moment the creatures could have been jokesters playing tricks on the local people. But the two silvery humanoids, according to the report by the Center for UFO Studies, began jumping about. Then, on their final jump, both lifted themselves into the sky and flew off like helicopters.

In eight cases, humanoids sighted in 1973 were reported to have kidnapped humans, often taking them aboard their ships and examining them closely before releasing them. Webb says that reports of abductions of this kind are becoming increasingly common.

Many of these abduction cases involve strange beings with remarkable similarities. They are generally remembered as short, silvery or silvery-gray, robotlike, and possessed of an unearthly ability to use brilliant lights that cause their victims to blank out.

In one case that has become well known among UFO investigators, a man was driving toward Cleveland, Ohio, late at night. An unusual light appeared beside his car. The lighted craft darted from one side of the road to the other, sometimes traveling at tremendous speed and sometimes hovering.

The driver remembered that he was traveling at seventy miles per hour. Then his mind went blank. But he apparently continued to drive, because an hour later, when he regained consciousness, he was driving at nearly ninety miles per hour.

This experience worried him. There was an hour of his life, an hour when he had been at the wheel of a speeding automobile, that he could not explain. The question of what had happened during that time would not let him rest. He visited a psychologist and allowed himself to be placed under hypnosis.

The psychologist questioned him and took him back to the night when he had seen the UFO. Gradually, his memory of the events of that hour returned. He recalled turning down a dark, quiet side road. There he was stopped by several unearthly figures whose eyes seemed to drive like X-rays into his brain. He spoke of being led into a craft, placed on a table, studied with brilliant penetrating lights. Then he was out of the craft, watching it lift off surrounded by a pale glowing light.

A few days later two Mississippi fishermen said they were taken aboard a strange UFO by three similar beings who seemed more like robots than living creatures. Both fishermen later recalled that these beings seemed to have no eyes—and that they floated rather than walked. The fishermen were examined, then released.

One Utah woman reported a frightening experience in which she was taken from her home by three unearthly beings. They carried her by her arms out of the house. Next she was inside a strange hospital-like room where several humanoids were at work. All of them were short, perhaps four or five feet tall, and they moved about almost like machines. Instead of hands they had claws. Their eyes were extremely large, and they had long "fishlike" mouths. They wore shiny silvery-blue uniforms.

Machines were attached to her, needles drew fluids from her, and she had the feeling that all her thoughts were easily known to her captors by mind reading. Her examination lasted nearly an hour. Then she was given a serum, which she thought was to blank out her memory, and returned to her home.

Studies of these mysteries continue. New UFOs are sighted and reported. Details accumulate. Anyone can help, anyone, that is, who happens to see an unidentified flying object. Police departments across the country can call the toll-free telephone number of the Center for UFO Studies. And their reports will be listened to carefully because, to the center, UFOs are serious business.

CHAPTER 4

Ghost Ships of the High Seas

There is, in New York City, a little one-room museum that keeps alive the memory of a ghost ship. You can visit this exhibit at the Atlantic Companies Building on Wall Street. There you will find a model of the doomed ship and some paintings and a few items salvaged from it. These tell the tragic story of the *Mary Celeste* and her final, mysterious voyage.

The haunting story of this famous ship first came to light on December 4, 1872. Captain David Read Morehouse stood on the deck of his little freighter, which was carrying a cargo of petroleum across the Atlantic. He studied the seas and the weather and before going to his cabin took one last look along the horizon.

Then he stopped and looked again. He squinted to

be sure of what he was seeing. Against the distant horizon was another ship. It was so far out that Captain Morehouse could tell neither its size nor its name. But he could see that it was sailing toward them.

As the silent ship drew closer, Captain Morehouse could see plainly that there was something unreal about her movements. She rolled aimlessly with the seas, as if no one stood at the wheel to keep her under control.

In addition, Captain Morehouse could see that her sails were trimmed in a manner that no captain of experience would permit in such a wind. When the two ships drew closer together the captain could make out her name. The drifting ship was the *Mary Celeste,* a small brigantine of 282 tons. She had departed from New York Harbor on November 7, 1872, with ten persons aboard. Among them were the captain's wife and their two-year-old daughter. It was not unusual for the captain to bring his family along on such voyages. His wife had brought her sewing machine and melodeon on what she expected to be an uneventful and pleasant trip. The *Mary Celeste*'s destination was Genoa, Italy, and her cargo consisted of seventeen hundred barrels of alcohol.

Captain Morehouse called out to the *Mary Celeste.* There was no answer. He called again and there was only silence in reply. After several attempts to get an answer, the captain spoke to his first mate, a skilled seaman named Oliver Deveau. "Take two men," he said, "and board her and see what the problem might be."

This painting shows how the *Mary Celeste* probably appeared to the first men to sight the ghost ship. (*The Atlantic Companies*)

A strange feeling settled over Deveau and the two seamen with him as they went aboard the drifting ship. There was a whispering of wind in the rigging and the irregular slap of waves against the wooden hull, but no sound of people anywhere.

The first mate returned to his own ship. "Sir, there's not a soul aboard her," he told Captain Morehouse. "She's like a ghost ship."

He told of what they had found in their brief inspection. They had found plenty of food and water, enough for any crossing. Those who had been aboard seemed to have left in a terrible hurry. Pipes and tobacco were left behind. Mrs. Brigg's clothes and even the child's toys were still on board. So were money and jewelry.

Deveau reported that he had checked the hold to see if the ship had taken water. He found only three and a half feet of water, not enough to be a threat to such a ship. Besides, her pumps were in top condition.

Nor was there evidence that the *Mary Celeste* had run into heavy storms. A vial of sewing-machine oil still stood upright where it had been set. Clothing left behind was still dry. Deveau found the ship's logbook and discovered that no entries had been made in the log after November 25. For the next nine days, the ship had wallowed through the seas on her own, drifting idly for at least 378 miles before the winds of the Atlantic.

Captain Morehouse faced a problem. His own crew was a small one. In addition to himself, there were only seven aboard the *Dei Gratia*. They were still many days from Gibraltar. But the captain decided to send Deveau and two seamen back aboard the *Mary Celeste*. Their orders were to sail her to Gibraltar. They made the trip in good time, arriving only half a day after the *Dei Gratia*.

There the ghost ship was taken into official custody. Captain Morehouse filed a claim for salvage.

In the weeks that followed, the ship without a crew became famous. No one could explain the mystery surrounding her. There was no report of her captain and crew. Her captain was Benjamin S. Briggs, who was known as a skilled and experienced sea captain. He was strict about the operation of his ship and expected the best efforts from his crew. But the lifeboats were missing from the *Mary Celeste* and so were the charts and navigation instruments. If the people aboard the *Mary Celeste* had been in the small boats, they might have been picked up at sea by some passing ship in the busy shipping lanes of the Atlantic.

Meanwhile, the courts tried to decide what to do about the ship. The little freighter had been built in Nova Scotia and had sailed for eleven years. During that time she had been sold a number of times.

There were some small things about the condition of the *Mary Celeste* that troubled the court. Experts scrambled over the ship searching for clues that might have been overlooked. There was a sword with a stain on the blade. The stain later proved to be rust. They found a piece of the ship's rail broken, but the court could not see that this had any sinister meaning. The mystery was as deep as ever.

When it completed its investigation, the court awarded the men of the *Dei Gratia* one fifth of the value of the *Mary Celeste* and her cargo; her cargo was seventeen hundred barrels of alcohol. This amounted to seventeen hundred pounds, or about eighty-three hundred dollars. The *Mary Celeste* was then given back to her owners.

But there was still the big unanswered question. Nothing had yet been seen of the crew of the *Mary Celeste*. And nothing ever was seen of them again, or of the lifeboats that had been on the ghost ship. They vanished completely. Several theories were advanced to account for the tragedy.

The chief investigator during the trials had pointed to Captain Morehouse and said that perhaps the crew of the *Dei Gratia* had killed the people on the *Mary Celeste* so that they could take the ship and claim it for salvage. But this did not make much sense. The cargo was not a highly valuable one. Besides, there was no real evidence that there had been a fight aboard the *Mary Celeste,* no upset furniture, broken dishes, or any of the other wreckage that would surely have been left by the crews of two ships fighting to the death. In addition, Captain Morehouse was known as an honest man. These charges were dismissed.

Other ideas were advanced. In the months and years

An artist's concept of how the *Mary Celeste* looked adrift on the Atlantic with no crew or passengers aboard. (*The Atlantic Companies*)

that followed, more and more people tried to explain the unbelievable case of a ship whose crew had completely vanished. Pirates? Once again, there had been no sign of a struggle on board. One of the barrels of alcohol was broken and perhaps there had been a flash fire, causing the captain and crew to panic and abandon their ship. But Captain Briggs was known as a cool-headed man, one not likely to panic easily.

For more than a hundred years the mystery of the *Mary Celeste* has gone unsolved. And it promises to remain one of the great unsolved sea mysteries for all time.

The remains of another mystery ghost ship are seen by tourists visiting the beach at Ocracoke Island. This island lies within the Cape Hatteras National Recreation Area along the seacoast of North Carolina. There, for more than a hundred miles, a strip of narrow, low-lying island protects the mainland from waves rolling in off the Atlantic. These sands reach out beneath the shallow water for miles in some places. Over the centuries hundreds of ships have been wrecked on the Outer Banks.

On the morning of January 31, 1921, Coast Guardsman C. P. Brady was on lookout at the Cape Hatteras Station. The winter sky was dark and stormy. The ocean was capped with white rolling waves chasing one another toward land. But the blustry winter scene with its rough seas and strong tide was no different from the ocean as Brady had seen it on many another winter dawn.

Then as the light of morning came he sighted a strange form against the dark clouds. He stared in disbelief. There, standing on Diamond Shoals, was a large ship, a five-masted schooner. All her sails were set. The southwest wind had driven her straight up onto the shoals, where she rested amid the rolling breakers.

Brady reported the schooner and by mid-morning two boats of rescue workers were approaching the wrecked ship. But the seas were too rough for the rescuers to move in close. All they could do was stay back a quarter of a mile from the mystery schooner and study it. They were still too far away to make out her name. But they could see that all the lifeboats were gone and that a ladder hung over the side of the ship.

The following day two Coast Guard cutters arrived, along with a wrecking tug, the *Rescue*. Still they could not approach the ship. She stood there waiting, silent and mysterious, for four days before the first crews could board her.

They found that high waves breaking over the deck had filled the hold with water. The ship had been battered so heavily that she would never sail again, even if she could be floated off the shoals. Now they knew the name of the unfortunate ship, the *Carroll A. Deering*.

She was not an old ship, but had been launched only two years earlier from the shipyards at Bath, Maine.

She was the last of a line of large schooners built by a prominent ship-building company, and she bore the name of the company owner's son. Her builders had been proud of her trim lines and her seaworthiness as she slid down into the waters of the bay to begin what they hoped would be a long and splendid life as a sailing vessel. She was 255 feet long and 44.3 feet wide, and her official papers registered her at 1,879 tons. On her final voyage she had been returning from Rio de Janeiro, headed for Norfolk, Virginia.

Nowhere in the ship could they find the slightest hint of what had happened to the crew, where they had gone, or why the lifeboats were not aboard. The searchers decided that those aboard the *Carroll A. Deering* had abandoned their ship with great speed. Pans still stood on the stoves, and food on the tables, ready to eat, was left untouched.

In the days that followed, wreckers removed items of value. The ghost ship was later dynamited. A section of her bow drifted southward along the Outer Banks and came to rest in the sands of Ocracoke Island.

Those who thought they knew what had happened to the ship's crew were only guessing. To some it seemed an open-and-shut case of piracy. Others said the crew had mutinied. Perhaps, however, as some within the Coast Guard believed, the entire crew of eleven men had abandoned the ship because it became evident that she was going to run aground in the storm; then, drifting out to sea in small open boats, they had perished.

Today, half a century after her ghostly arrival on Diamond Shoals, nobody yet knows what caused her to wreck.

The *Rubicon* was a cargo ship out of Cuba and she would not be remembered today by many people except that she too joined the ranks of the ghost ships. Navy observers on regular patrol, October 22, 1944, first sighted her adrift thirty miles southeast of Key Largo, Florida.

The observers flew close to her and saw no sign of life aboard. Drifting idly on the sea with no night lights, she was a menace to other ships. There was also the possibility that there were crewmen aboard who needed help. The naval observers radioed the Coast Guard and reported the location of the *Rubicon*.

Within a few minutes the Coast Guard had two of its fast patrol boats on the way to check out the reported ship. They found her precisely where the Navy crew had reported, but as they drew closer they could see that another ship had arrived ahead of them. Under the law of the sea a ship without a crew can be claimed for salvage, and the *Rubicon* had been discovered by the captain of an American boat, who already had her under tow.

The ship towing the *Rubicon* was joined by the two Coast Guard boats and all three escorted her into the harbor at Miami.

But the mystery of the Cuban ghost ship was never solved. Those who went aboard found no living human, only a small dog weak from hunger. The ship was inspected for signs of violence and no evidence was found that there had been a struggle. The lifeboats were gone, with no explanation of why the crew had departed. Judging from the ship's log, the *Rubicon* had drifted aimlessly without a crew for two weeks. That is about all that was ever learned of what prompted the *Rubicon*'s crew to abandon ship, leaving her to join the *Carroll Deering* and the *Mary Celeste* as a mystery ghost ship of the open seas.

CHAPTER 5

The Bermuda Triangle

With a map of the Atlantic Ocean, and a ruler, almost anyone can outline the Bermuda Triangle, the "triangle of death." Starting at Miami, Florida, draw a line northeast to Bermuda. Then draw another line from Miami southeast to San Juan, Puerto Rico. Connect these lines with a third line and you are looking at a wedge of ocean where hundreds of people have met tragic unexplained death.

Beginning in 1945, the number of cases of disappearances within the Bermuda Triangle skyrocketed. More than one hundred planes and ships have now disappeared from the air and waters of the Triangle. With them more than a thousand people have van-

On December 5, 1945, five Grumman Avenger aircraft on a routine naval training flight out of Florida vanished without a trace inside the Bermuda Triangle. (*Official U. S. Navy Photograph*)

ished, leaving not a hint of what might have happened. No wreckage has been found, no oil slicks, no bodies. Nothing but the empty and mysterious sea with its endless waves rolling and surging toward distant unseen shores.

Within the Bermuda Triangle, rescue teams have staged searches as complex and sophisticated as any in history. Few such searches could have been more complete, or less successful, than the hunt for the five U. S. Navy Grumman TBM Avenger torpedo bombers that lifted off the runways at Fort Lauderdale, Florida, at 2:10 P.M. on December 5, 1945.

Each of the five planes was checked out in the usual detailed manner. Each carried a full load of fuel, enough for five to five and a half hours. Aboard each of the bombers was all the usual emergency gear, including radios, emergency rations, inflatable life rafts. Not everyone was eager to start on this flight. One crew member requested permission to remain behind. He had a disturbing feeling that he should not make the run. He was excused and nobody was assigned to fill his place. According to the records of the official Naval Board of Inquiry, the training officer slated to take the flight out also asked to be relieved. He did not say why, but did request that he be relieved. There was, however, no other officer available for the flight, so the request was denied. The five flying officers and nine enlisted men suited up and climbed into their planes.

For the first hour after takeoff, everything appeared to go according to plan. The flight leader was in radio contact with his other planes and these messages were heard in the tower back at Fort Lauderdale. The messages were routine. The five planes had droned along over the ocean steadily, made their practice bombing run, and were expected to be heading back to Fort Lauderdale.

Then the radioman in the control tower at Fort Lauderdale began to receive strange messages that made no sense. The flight leader and other pilots were talking in a confused and garbled manner. The fliers were unable to determine their location. Their compasses were broken. They could see nothing that would give them an idea of where they were. The tower lost radio contact with the planes.

According to an information sheet issued by the Navy, "Attempts to establish communications and to reach the troubled flight were in vain. All radio contact was lost before the exact nature of the trouble or the location of the flight could be determined. Indications are that the flight became lost somewhere east of the Florida peninsula and was unable to determine a course to return to base." The flight was never heard from again and no trace of the planes was ever found. It is assumed that they crashed at sea, possibly after running out of fuel. It is known that the fuel carried by the aircraft would have been completely exhausted by 8 P.M.

Back at the naval station, word of the strange events

surrounding the training flight flashed around the air base. A large rescue plane, the *Martin Mariner*—or flying boat—was warmed up and its thirteen-man crew climbed aboard.

A few minutes after the rescue plane had left the runway, heading out to sea, the tower received the last message ever heard from it. This was a report of strong winds. Now all six planes were lost. None of them was ever heard from again and to this day there is still speculation about what might have caused them to vanish over the Atlantic. Through the following days more than three hundred aircraft, various naval vessels, and many privately owned boats and planes joined in the search. The ocean had swallowed all clues to the mystery. The searchers found not a single piece of wreckage.

These were not the first cases of planes and ships vanishing in that section of the Atlantic. Earlier that year, another naval plane, a four-engine craft carrying fifteen men, had flown out over the ocean from Miami on a standard training flight. The plane left just after midnight. Nobody knows what happened to it or its crew.

Another plane disappeared July 3, 1947. This one was a U. S. Army cargo transport, a two-engine C-54 carrying a crew of six. Its flight plan called for it to travel from Bermuda to Palm Beach, Florida. But its radio went off the air. By mid-afternoon when the C-54 should have been returning to its base, there was no sign of it and no sound in the sky. Again a giant sea search was mounted.

For the next four days, planes and ships covered every part of the area. They found nothing.

There have been many other equally mysterious disappearances within the Triangle. One of these occurred six months later when a plane carrying thirty-two passengers was en route from San Juan, the capital of Puerto Rico, to Miami. The plane never arrived and no trace was ever found of the plane or the people aboard.

But even before aircraft became a common method of travel there were mysterious events occurring within this section of the Atlantic. The U.S.S. *Cyclops* was a Navy ship, 542 feet long. She sailed from Barbados in March 1918, headed for Norfolk, Virginia. On board were 309 people, 73 of them passengers.

During the time she was en route to Norfolk there were no reported storms. But the ship lost contact with all other ships and failed to arrive on time.

The search that the Navy mounted for the big supply ship was a gigantic effort. Orders went out from Washington to miss no possible place that might yield clues of what had happened to the ship and the people aboard her. Search vessels poked into remote harbors, scoured the ocean route of the *Cyclops,* and checked out the islands large and small. Still no evidence was discovered, not the first bit.

People did more than search for the ship; they also

speculated on the cause of her strange vanishing act. America was at war that year and some thought that German submarines might have accounted for the disappearance of the *Cyclops*. But two facts argued against this. First, the search did not turn up any evidence of the wreckage that such a sinking would almost certainly have left. Besides, German records were examined and there were no German submarines operating at that time in that part of the Atlantic and there were no mines placed there.

There were equally strong arguments against the possibilities that the *Cyclops* had been the victim of an explosion or had been taken by pirates. Evidence of these acts would almost certainly have been found. To this day, the tragedy of the *Cyclops* is considered simply one more on the long list of unexplained disappearances within the Bermuda Triangle.

The list includes a number of small craft operated by private owners. It also includes some that, like the *Mary Celeste,* have been found without their crews. Many of these losses occurred when weather was excellent, as far as anyone knows, and when there was no other reason to think the ships were facing danger. "The disappearance of this ship has been one of the most baffling mysteries in the annals of the Navy," said a release from the Navy Office of Information. "All attempts to locate her have proved unsuccessful."

What happened to the lost aircraft and ships of the Bermuda Triangle? Why have so many vanished and left behind no sign of wreckage or even a film of oil shining on the ocean's surface? Is some strange, unexplained force responsible? The Navy takes the official stand that this is a completely normal region of the ocean.

About all that is known for certain is that a large number of mysterious disappearances have occurred within a relatively limited section of the ocean. There have been tragedies elsewhere on the ocean, many of them, as long as men have traveled the seas. But the concentration of cases within the Triangle keeps people speculating about possible causes. There may be some entirely logical explanation for all these disasters at sea. But so far no one has found a clue to it. The Triangle of Death guards its mystery.

CHAPTER 6

Big Birds of Texas

In February 1976 a teacher at a Texas rural school had the scare of her life. While driving on a country road she suddenly realized that a gigantic flying creature was diving at her car. It cast a shadow covering the width of the road. She then saw a second flying creature, apparently the mate of the first one.

Thoroughly shaken by her unearthly experience, the teacher drove on to the schoolhouse. She went to the library and began pulling out volumes of the encyclopedia, looking for pictures of prehistoric monsters. She examined all the pictures of dinosaurs she could find until she came to what she was certain she had seen flying over the road. Now she was more upset than ever. She was convinced that she had seen a flying reptile that has been extinct for millions of years.

Her school principal begged her not to tell anyone. He was worried. Students might panic. Parents would keep their children home behind locked doors.

But word did get out. Two other teachers also reported seeing one of the winged giants that day. Just as it had with the first teacher, the beast swooped low over their cars.

"It was the biggest thing I've ever seen alive," one of them told a reporter. "It's just unreal. I don't know how it could have survived all those millions of years and still be flying around here. It all happened so fast and it was such a shock you think you are seeing things. It was just enormous and frightening."

These were not the only reports of a mysterious winged giant loose in southern Texas at that time. There was a long list of sightings. Nobody was sure what these creatures might be. They were all known simply as "Big Bird." Every day there seemed to be fresh reports arriving in the offices of the Texas Parks and Wildlife Department. "We were fascinated," said one state wildlife official.

Perhaps the first to see Big Bird was police officer Arturo Padilla of San Benito, an experienced hunter and outdoorsman. Driving his police car just before dawn, Padilla saw the broad-winged bird in the beam of his headlights. There were few vehicles on the streets except an occasional police cruiser.

A few minutes later another police officer, Homer Galvan, saw the giant. He remembered it as a black silhouette gliding through the air. "It never did flap its wings," he told reporters. He thought its wingspread must have been at least twelve feet. He added that if he had the right opportunity he intended to shoot it.

Next to turn in a report of Big Bird was Alverico Guajardo, who lived in a mobile home on the edge of Brownsville. While eating dinner at about nine-thirty on a January night, Guajardo heard a thumping against the side of his trailer. He eased out the door. A monstrous bird was standing in his yard. He hurried to his car and switched on the headlights. The lights revealed the most frightening animal Guajardo had ever seen. "I was scared," he admitted to a reporter. "It's like a bird but it's not a bird. That animal is not from this world." Guajardo especially remembered the oversized eyes and the bill, which extended three or four feet. It stood there in the glare of the headlights and issued a loud rumbling bird call that Guajardo had never heard before. After he had studied the creature from a distance of fifteen feet for several minutes, the bird turned and did not fly but walked away, melting into the blackness.

Reports continued to come from along the Rio Grande Valley. One television station broadcast pictures of a Big Bird track twelve inches long. The footprint was found in freshly plowed soil.

People throughout southern Texas became increasingly excited. A radio station offered a thousand-dollar reward to anyone who captured Big Bird. In Abilene a wealthy oil man offered another five thousand dollars. Through the following nights men took their guns from the racks and fanned out over the countryside. They flashed their lights into dark hollows and up toward the Texas sky, hoping for a glimpse of the elusive flying monster.

This flurry of activity quickly brought the Texas Parks and Wildlife Department to the defense of Big Bird, whatever it might be. Officials said they could not be sure of what the citizens along the Rio Grande were seeing, but if the animal was real it would almost certainly be very rare and therefore on the endangered-species list. This would bring it full government protection. Bounty hunters trying to kill or harass it could end up in jail.

In addition, the state wildlife officials were concerned about other big birds of Texas, ones they knew were flying around. These included vultures, sandhill cranes, brown pelicans, the rare whooping cranes, wild geese, and others that might get shot by mistake. Excited Big Bird hunters could easily make a serious error and kill a protected bird. "All birds," the officials announced, "are protected by state or federal law."

But after two months of excitement the search for Big Bird gradually came to an end. "Apparently," said state wildlife officials, "the furor has subsided." Still nobody knew what Big Bird might really have been or

Scientists at the American Museum of Natural History in New York constructed this model of the giant pterosaur discovered in Texas to show the size of the creature. The wingspread is fifty-one feet. (*Courtesy of the American Museum of Natural History*)

where it had come from. Most people had their own ideas. There was speculation that it was actually an escaped South American condor, a brown pelican, a great blue heron, a prehistoric monster that had gone undiscovered, or a creature from outer space. The answer may never be known, but along the Rio Grande, Big Bird will not be easily forgotten. Many people believe it may show up again at any time.

The story of Big Bird reminded some of the startling discovery earlier in Big Bend National Park. Far back in a section of the desert where park visitors seldom go, Douglas A. Lawson, with a scientific permit from the .U. S. Park Service, had been exploring a sandstone outcropping when he came upon the remains of giant wing bones. The following spring Lawson came back and this time he brought along his professor. They soon agreed that what Lawson had discovered were the fossilized bones of a pterosaur, the first ever found in west Texas.

These newly discovered bones were carefully compared with the fossils of other pterosaurs found in Jordan and in the state of Wyoming. The Texas flying reptile of more than sixty million years ago was the largest of all, indeed it was the largest flying animal ever known on earth! It had a wingspread of fifty-one feet.

There remained a number of unanswered questions about the giant flying reptile Lawson had discovered. Scientists debated whether it had actually flown by flapping its giant batlike wings or simply launched itself from high hills and soared about the countryside.

In addition, there was the question of what the ancient "flying lizard" ate. It lived far from lakes of those times, so it is doubtful that it depended on fish. In view of the length of its neck, ". . . long enough to probe a dinosaur carcass," as Lawson wrote in *Science*, it might have been a carrion feeder. This remarkable animal's ability to soar was probably much like that of today's vultures.

Whether there is some relationship between the news stories of Lawson's giant flying reptile and the later reports of Big Bird cannot be known. After a few months the excitement over both creatures died down. But Texas, and the world, may not yet have seen the last of Big Bird.

CHAPTER 7

Mystery of Oak Island

If you were to go to Nova Scotia in eastern Canada you could visit Oak Island. You might think at first that there is little to make this island famous. It is only half a mile wide and about a mile long. Besides, there is nothing impressive-looking about it. There are thousands of islands along the east coast of North America that might seem just as interesting. But Oak Island has been famous for nearly two hundred years. It is to this day the scene of one of the most perplexing mysteries anywhere.

This story begins in 1795 with sixteen-year-old Dan McGinnis. Dan spent much of his spare time hunting, fishing, and exploring the woods along the coast of

Oak Island, shown here, is the scene of one of the greatest lost-treasure mysteries of all time. (*Photo: Nova Scotia Communication and Information Centre*)

Nova Scotia. Often Dan would row a small boat to remote corners of Mahone Bay. This was how he visited Oak Island one day.

Nobody lived on Oak Island then. It was a wild, sandy place except for a grove of large oak trees on one edge of it.

Dan pulled his boat up on the sand where it would be secure and hiked into the oak grove. There, as legend tells it, he sat down beneath a tall oak tree to rest and cool off. But as he sat there he began to notice the strange, unnatural appearance of this place. Beneath one of the biggest of all the oak trees the earth was sunken in a bowl-shaped depression several feet deep. Dan looked up into the tree. A heavy limb held a part of a pulley that was centered directly above the hole.

As he studied the evidence, Dan became more and more excited. He began recalling stories he had heard about Oak Island. One old lady in Chester had said her grandmother believed there was a curse on the place because she had seen strange lights floating low over the island in the darkness of night. She also said that people had rowed over to investigate and never come back.

The next day Dan McGinnis returned to Oak Island. This time he brought two companions, Jack Smith and Anthony Vaughan. They carried shovels with them and, convinced that they had found the site of a buried treasure, began digging.

The farther they dug into the hole, the more excited

they became. Hour after hour they continued to dig. By evening they had cleaned out the shaft to a depth of ten feet. There they made an exciting discovery. Their shovels, after cutting into the soft earth, had been stopped by something so hard they could not dent it. They carefully cleaned away the earth until they had uncovered a platform of heavy wooden planks laid side by side across the shaft.

That night they took vows of silence and went home convinced that they were about to dig up a fabulous buried treasure. The first light of dawn was scarcely touching the calm waters of the harbor when the three treasure seekers slipped out of their homes and pushed their boat quietly off toward Oak Island.

They worked the planks free one at a time and heaved them up out of the pit. Beneath this floor of heavy timbers they would surely find chests of gold, silver, and precious stones. They worked faster and faster and barely spoke in their excitement.

But they found no treasure, only more earth. The presence of the timbers, however, was enough to convince them that someone had once dug a deep pit here beneath the giant oak tree. What reason would anyone have except to bury treasure? They dug on.

Days later they had dug down another ten feet. There they found a second platform of timbers, like the first one. Once again they cleaned the earth from the planks and lifted the heavy pieces from the pit.

This was no time to stop. How deep could anyone

dig to bury a treasure? They were now at twenty feet and surely must be getting close.

Day after day, all summer long, they went back to the island. Foot by foot they deepened their treasure pit. No longer could they throw the earth up out of the hole with their shovels, so they rigged a bucket with ropes and pulleys to lift it to the surface. They were still there digging when the icy winds of winter stopped their work for the year. But by this time they had lowered the shaft to thirty feet. There again they found another platform of timbers.

The following spring they dug again. But now they needed help if their treasure search was to continue. They needed money, so they had to stop and take other jobs. For many years the three friends continued their trips to the island and dug in the pit whenever they could. Eventually, both Smith and McGinnis married and took their brides to live in small homes they had built on Oak Island beside the pit in which their hopes were buried.

There on the island Dan McGinnis and his wife raised their family. Four generations of McGinnises have lived on the island, always hoping to reach the treasure, always thinking and planning about how best to uncover the hidden riches.

But the search had grown steadily more difficult. Since Dan McGinnis first discovered the pit on Oak Island, other treasure hunters have gone there to unearth its riches. There have been at least fifteen such parties

For generation after generation, frustrated treasure hunters have tried to reach the bottom of the "money pit" on Oak Island, Nova Scotia. (*Photo: Nova Scotia Communication and Information Centre*)

of treasure hunters and together they have spent more than two million dollars. Nine people have lost their lives in the search for the treasure of Oak Island.

Nine years after the three friends first worked the pit, a company brought in mining equipment and the three pioneers worked for the company. Now more than ever, they were sure they were about to learn the secret of Oak Island. The shaft was going deeper into the earth. This company continued digging for the next two years.

By the time they gave up in disgust, the shaft was ninety-five feet deep. About every ten feet the diggers had found a new platform. In addition to the heavy plank floors built into the pit, there was, at the fifty-five-foot level, a layer of putty like that carried in wooden ships for waterproofing cracks. Another layer was of charcoal, and a third was of a coarse fiber that investigators believed must have come from the tropics.

It is also said that at a depth of ninety feet they uncovered a remarkable stone with symbols carved on it. Nobody could decipher the marks. The stone disappeared many years later, about 1904, and perhaps nothing more will ever be learned from it or about it.

Then came a Saturday evening when the pit was ninety-five feet deep. The crew quit digging until Monday, but first they had probed the soft earth at the bottom of the pit with an iron rod. Five feet down lay another wooden platform, and perhaps it would be beneath this layer of wood, at a depth of one hundred feet, that the treasure would be found.

But Monday morning brought a new surprise. Over the weekend the pit had flooded with water. It stood within thirty-five feet of the top. They brought buckets to bail out the hole. But for every bucket removed another bucket flowed back in from somewhere. All their work did not lower the level by as much as a cup.

Then someone thought of digging another shaft nearby. Perhaps this would take them to the level of the treasure. The workers dug a new pit 110 feet deep. Next they dug sideways toward the old pit. Logically enough, this let water flow from the old pit to the new one and soon both were filled to the same level.

Time passed. The three original diggers grew old. But not rich. Yet they never lost faith in their "money pit." Through the years, the story of the Oak Island treasure spread. Others dreamed of trying their own ideas for recovering the riches of Oak Island. The next big effort came in 1849.

Using modern methods, this group of investors sank a number of shafts. Again they had trouble with water flooding the shafts. One idea was to bring in a drill and use it to explore deeper into the earth than they had been able to dig. This might at least answer some questions. The idea was to bring the drill up frequently and inspect its blades for clues.

First the bit worked through another layer of oak planks. Then it came to what seemed to be a box of loose metal. Now the treasure hunters were convinced that they had reached the hidden riches. It is said that the drill came up at one time with three pieces of gold chain stuck to it.

But this company of investors ran out of money and still there was the unsolved problem of the water. Finally, after months of hope, work, and despair, they gave up and left Oak Island.

There were other treasure hunters trying for the prize of Oak Island in following years. In 1909 even Franklin D. Roosevelt, future President of the United States, invested money in a company that thought it had the perfect plan to recover the treasure. It told those who invested in it that it expected to recover ten million dollars. Furthermore, it had bright new ideas on how to get down there where the money waited. This company lasted two months before giving up and leaving Oak Island.

During the 1960s others took up the exploration. They studied the water coming into the pits and decided that this flooding was all part of an elaborate plan engineered by whoever had buried the treasure. The water in the pit was salt water coming in from the ocean. A series of tunnels was said to route it into the treasure pit. The belief was that those who had built these tunnels had somehow designed them so they would open, flooding the shaft, if anyone approached the treasure. Those who knew the secret would know how to reach the buried treasure without opening the pit to the sea water. If this was true, the plan had worked perfectly.

Modern drilling equipment also failed to solve the riddle of Oak Island. (*Photo: Nova Scotia Communication and Information Centre*)

Many times in the years since, others have gone out to Oak Island to seek the elusive treasure. They have taken to the little island practically every aid they could think of. Some have tried hydraulic pumps, others the most modern drills, roaring bulldozers, and heavy charges of dynamite.

Meanwhile, speculation continues about what, if anything, is hidden down there. The most common guess is that Captain Kidd, perhaps history's most famous pirate, had used Oak Island as his safety-deposit vault and hidden riches of untold value. Some insisted that beneath Oak Island the crown jewels of France were buried, or chests of ancient South American treasure planted by Spanish looters.

Perhaps the most tragic days of this long, long treasure hunt came after Robert Restall went to Oak Island in 1960. Restall was a Canadian who had worked as a motorcycle stunt rider in European circuses. But in the back of his mind were stories he had heard as a boy about the mystery of Oak Island. He retired and took his family back to Canada.

Through the next five years the Restalls and their children lived in a shack on the island, digging, thinking, searching, hoping, dreaming. But year by year they fed treasure into the pit instead of taking it out. The pit was swallowing their savings.

Then one day in 1965, Robert Restall lowered himself into the pit as he had done many times to work with a pump on a platform down at water level. Per-

Today the mystery of Oak Island is as great as ever. (*Photo: Nova Scotia Communication and Information Centre*)

haps the fumes from the pump overcame him. He lost consciousness and fell from the platform into the water.

His eldest son rushed down to help him; he too was overcome and fell to his death in the water. Two men who worked on Restall's crew went into the shaft to rescue the boy and his father. The crewmen too, died. The treasure pit of Oak Island had claimed four human victims in a single day. And nobody was any closer to finding the fabulous treasure.

About the same time, Daniel Blankenship, a Miami real-estate developer, became interested in Oak Island. He bought shares in the company Restall had formed. Blankenship took up the search, and one thing he did was start digging a completely new shaft two hundred feet northeast of the main hole. This shaft reached a large pit far beneath the island.

He next lowered a closed-circuit television camera into the hole. On that first attempt to televise the contents of the pit, Blankenship believes, he saw part of a chest. He is also convinced that he saw one other object floating in the dark water, a human hand. The hand never has been explained.

But there is much about Oak Island that remains to be explained. Whatever its secret, the island has held it safe against all human searchers for nearly two centuries. And perhaps no one ever will solve the mystery of Oak Island.

CHAPTER 8

The Gold Nobody Can Find

At this very moment there probably are gold hunters scrambling through rocky canyons in the rugged dry mountains east of Phoenix, Arizona. Prospectors have come here for centuries, carrying their pickaxes, driven by their dreams of fantastic riches. They look behind the boulders, dig in the dry beds of the streams, and follow all manner of tips and leads. They pray for guidance. They carry good-luck charms. They think about all the searchers who have already failed to find the hidden treasure of the Superstition Mountains, the world-famous Lost Dutchman Gold Mine.

It is a dream that has brought thousands of them to this rugged country and led many to their deaths. But the Lost Dutchman Mine is still lost, its legendary riches locked in the mountains, its riddle unsolved.

Many an engineer doubts that the gleaming metal is there at all, in good quantity. But who can be sure? Legend tells of a great vein of gold locked deep within the rocky walls of the Superstition Mountains, riches beyond the dreams of mortals.

Some accounts say that the Indians knew of the gold for centuries before the arrival of Europeans. But there is no evidence to support this belief. Others insist that the earliest white people to locate the riches were the conquistadores of Coronado. But it is known that the troops led by Coronado in search of gold almost certainly did not go to the Superstition Mountains.

The real legend of the Lost Dutchman Mine appears to begin with a wealthy family of Mexicans of Spanish descent, the Peraltas. Their story has the king of Spain granting to Don Miguel Peralta de Cordova eighteen thousand square miles of desert. This grant covered much of southern Arizona and New Mexico, including the present site of Phoenix and the Superstition Mountains to the east.

But the Peraltas did not live in this harsh desert country far from the refinements to which they were accustomed. It was one thing to own the land, another to occupy it. Instead they built their ranches in Mexico and did very well there. For half a century following the gift from the king in 1748, the Peraltas grew wealthy from ranching and from mining silver.

Then the mines they worked began to run out of silver. Perhaps because of this, the younger men in the

Somewhere in the rugged desert country of the Superstition Mountains may be a waiting fortune. (*Photo: U. S. Forest Service*)

family began at last to take trips northward to look over the family holdings. One of these trips took them to the Superstition Mountains.

On these journeys the Peraltas and the laborers they brought with them were not alone, because the land they had been given by the king of Spain had already been given to the Apaches by the Great Spirit. But on that first trip the Indians did not attack them and the Peraltas returned to their home with an impressive amount of gold.

In the following years they repeated the journey. And each trip yielded more gold. They were said to have opened eight mines, and perhaps more. In 1847 the Peraltas decided to make a grand journey and bring out more of their gold than they had harvested on all their earlier trips. Their long caravan consisted of four hundred men and two hundred pack animals. Surely the Apaches would not attack so large a force.

From their hidden outposts the Apaches watched the column approaching from miles away. They studied the men and animals winding through the narrowing canyons into the heart of the Superstition Mountains, land they considered sacred. Word went out through the Apache nation. Warriors began assembling from many directions.

Secure in their numbers, the Mexicans dug their gold and packed it onto their beasts. The long lines formed again and the march to the south began. Still the silent Apaches waited. They allowed the miners to come out of the rocky canyons and into more open country.

Then the Indians began their attack. Some say that the gold was scattered everywhere about the desert during that fight. The mules ran off and the Apaches killed nearly all the Mexicans.

This makes an interesting story. But more-sober-minded historians point out that those who have visited the site have found no pieces of metal or other souvenirs. Some even speculate that the whole story of the Peraltas is fiction, not fact.

But the Dutchman for whom the lost mine was named was real, although he was not Dutch. His name was Jacob Waltz and he first came to Arizona about 1870. With him came his friend, Jacob Weiser. Their families had come to this country from Germany in 1848 and settled in St. Louis, Missouri. In those days people from Germany were often called Dutch.

For some time the two friends worked at various jobs around Arizona. But not until they set off into the mountains to work for themselves did the stories about their activities begin. There was nothing especially noteworthy about either of the men except that whenever one of them came to town, he would pay for his purchases with pure gold carried in a handy pocket pouch. This alone was enough to attract attention on the frontier.

It was also enough to send curious trackers lurking behind either Waltz or Weiser as he made his way back toward the hills. But somehow nobody ever succeeded in following them farther than the edge of the mountains. It was as if the Superstitions swallowed them up and nothing would be seen of them again until one of them arrived unannounced in town with his trusty bag of nuggets.

The story of the two men is usually tied to two Mexicans whom they are said to have found working a mine deep in the Superstitions. Waltz and Weiser shot the two, according to this legend, and took over their mine.

Eventually Weiser disappeared. Some said he had been shot by his partner. Others credited the act to the Apaches.

Waltz lived until 1891, when he died a. nonviolent death in bed at his little home on the edge of Phoenix. As an old man, Waltz was not living as one might expect of the owner of a fabulously rich gold mine. But not all people who acquire great wealth change their life styles, so this alone can hardly be taken as evidence that Waltz did *not* have a gold mine.

Through his later years Waltz was friendly with a local widow, Mrs. Helena Thomas, who operated a small shop in Phoenix. At one time Mrs. Thomas was badly in need of funds to save her business from bankruptcy and Waltz came to her rescue. He handed her a pouch of gold ore, which she dispatched to San Francisco for smelting. This ore yielded fourteen hundred dollars and Waltz gave one thousand dollars of it to Mrs. Thomas.

In addition, Waltz promised Mrs. Thomas that when spring came he would lead her and her fifteen-year-old foster son, Reiny Petrasch, into the mountains. He would show them where he had buried cases of gold. But Waltz, past eighty, was failing in health. When spring came he could no longer follow the trails up into the Superstitions. Before he died, however, he spent hours describing to Mrs. Thomas and Reiny the landmarks by which they could recognize his gold mine.

Following the death of her friend Waltz, Mrs. Thomas searched the mountains many times. Her business faltered. Her money ran out. So did her luck. In the rocky canyons of the Superstitions she never was able to sort out the landmarks that might have led her to the Lost Dutchman Mine.

Meanwhile, Reiny continued the search, trying to follow the clues passed on to him by Waltz. Many prospectors have since taken special notice of the area where Reiny concentrated his digging. This was near a famous rock formation known as Weaver's Needle, in La Barge Canyon. But, like others who have sought the Lost Dutchman Mine, Reiny failed. He died blind, poor, and disillusioned.

Meanwhile, the search for the legendary mine attracted more and more people. Writers were picking up the story and repeating it, even adding details and fresh angles. People read of the Lost Dutchman Mine and many headed for Arizona.

Today, the Superstition Mountains lie within the Superstition Wilderness Area in the Tonto National Forest. Rangers patrol the lonely canyons. They know that

Weaver's Needle, shown in this picture of the Superstition Wilderness in the Tonto National Forest, is a prominent landmark for treasure seekers pursuing the legend of the lost gold mine. (*Photo: U. S. Forest Service*)

most visitors go no more than a mile or two into the area where Peralta, Waltz, and others are said to have found gold. Vehicles are not permitted and helicopters are not allowed to make landings. In addition, the canyons are so rugged and the faintly marked trails so rocky that only the most daring and rugged explorers, those who understand the desert back country, can safely travel there.

But the search goes on. The Forest Service does not stop the prospectors. They are free to go into the Superstitions by foot or by pack train. And once there, they are free to prospect. They are even allowed by law to stake a mining claim. But they are not allowed to use power tools.

Waltz often said that his mine would be difficult to find. Whenever he left it, he went to great trouble to hide it. The mine shaft was covered and camouflaged. This he did every time he left, including the last time. Today it remains hidden. But prospectors still come, hoping to solve the mystery of the Superstition Mountains and the lost gold mine.

CHAPTER 9

The Trail of Bigfoot

Anyone might be afraid of Bigfoot. The creature stands taller than a man, weighs several times more, is covered all over with dark shaggy hair, and walks along with an apelike gait, swinging long, clublike arms that could kill a man, or maybe an ox, with a single blow.

But Bigfoot is famous for his gentleness. As nearly as anyone can learn, no human has been purposely harmed by one of these famous monsters. Bigfoot, instead of rushing at a person, may stand quietly, in the shadows at the edge of the forest, curiously studying the person. Then when he knows he has been seen he simply slips into the shadows and vanishes as harmlessly as a baby. He does not growl, yell, hiss, snort, or bare his teeth.

In spite of all this, Bigfoot attracts more attention than any other monster with the possible exception of that creature in Loch Ness. Bigfoot is not new to the forested country of Washington, Oregon, California, and British Columbia. Indians told of seeing these elusive animals long ago. They had their own name for Bigfoot; they called him Sasquatch.

Until recently Bigfoot, or Sasquatch, has been left to his own to roam harmlessly through the woods. But now, dedicated monster searchers are combing the wilderness, alert for the slightest glimpse of the great hairy giant and hoping to solve the long-standing mystery of what Bigfoot is and where he came from.

At the turn of this century Bigfoot was already a mystifying creature. Timber workers and trappers living in lonely wilderness cabins reported seeing "a terrible monster." In 1904 an Oregon newspaper said that for a decade stories of Bigfoot had been filtering in from the forests. Some people said the beast was a wild man. Others insisted it was like no man anywhere. The newspaper, the Lane County *Leader,* reported the case of two men sitting by their fire one night when they heard heavy footsteps around the cabin. The creature outside grasped a corner of the cabin and shook it until it rattled. This was too much. One of the men threw open the door in time to see Bigfoot running away. The man fired at it with his rifle, but he missed.

A few weeks later Bigfoot made another appearance. This time it arrived at five in the morning and shook

Bigfoot is said to favor the deep dark forests of the Pacific Northwest, such as this section of the famous redwood forests of northern California. (*Photo: George Laycock*)

the door of another cabin. This brought the occupants tumbling out of their beds. One man, rifle in hand, bravely jerked open the cabin door. Again the monster was fired upon, and again it was missed. Bigfoot turned and hurled a large rock at the gunman. One could hardly blame him. But, he missed too.

The newspaper editor said that an average Bigfoot ". . . is about seven feet high, has broad hands and feet, and his body is covered by a thick growth of hair. In short, he looks like the devil."

Unlike some monsters, Bigfoot did not disappear as time passed. Instead, more and more people said they saw it. There are doubters. Among them are numerous scientists. But other scientists believe Bigfoot may really be out there lurking deep in the forests. Those who think there is no such animal are quick to bring up puzzling questions. Why has no dead Bigfoot ever been found, they want to know. Why have not more people seen them? How does Bigfoot stay hidden?

The believers have their answers ready. They describe the vastness of the forests in the Pacific Northwest. In this they have a good argument. For mile after mile the blanket of towering trees stretches across mountains and over valleys. Hikers, hunters, and fishermen may walk the trails. But seldom do they penetrate the heart of the deepest wilderness. There are hundreds of square miles where few people ever go. And even if hikers were to invade the secret hiding places of Bigfoot, there is every reason to believe that a creature that wanted to stay hidden could easily do so.

Besides, Bigfoot is a creature of the night, say those who claim to know him best, a shy, elusive, harmless beast that has survived only by keeping himself hidden from people. Bigfoot is also said to be a rare animal. This means, simply, that there are few opportunities for encounters between people and Bigfoot.

Some doubters say that because scientists do not already know about Bigfoot there must not be such a beast. There is no Bigfoot anywhere in a zoo or museum and no one has yet made scientific measurements of the body of one. But this alone may not be sufficient reason for saying flatly that such a creature could not be out there slipping through the forests. New discoveries are still being made. In 1972 an entirely unknown tribe of humans, the Tasaday, was found in the jungles of the Philippines. The coelacanth, a primitive fish believed extinct for seventy million years, was found alive and well off the coast of Africa in 1938. On the Hawaiian island of Maui, two college students recently discovered a bird entirely new to science, a bird that has no near relatives anywhere in the world.

If there is a Bigfoot, it is already rare, and man has a responsibility to protect rare and endangered wild creatures. In Skamania County, Washington, in 1969, the Board of County Commissioners passed an ordinance to protect Bigfoot. The county commissioners explained that there had been recent evidence indicating the "possible existence of a nocturnal primate mammal described as an apelike creature or a subspecies of *Homo sapiens. . . .*" These reports, according to the commissioners, have attracted hunters. Anyone convicted of killing one of the mystery animals can be fined ten thousand dollars and imprisoned for up to five years in the county jail.

One man who is determined to find the mysterious Bigfoot is Peter Byrne, an ex-professional big game hunter with experience in both Africa and Asia. "The hunt for Bigfoot began for me," he said in his book *The Search for Bigfoot,* "in the winter of 1959." He was then living in the high, cold Himalayas of Nepal, searching for the Yeti, which is believed to be similar to Sasquatch.

This search was paid for by a Texas oilman. Then the oilman began hearing about Bigfoot. He asked Byrne to drop his search for the Abominable Snowman and fly to America. As a result, Byrne switched his hunting grounds from Nepal to Oregon.

Byrne's search ended, however, when his Texas friend died. He packed up and returned to Nepal, and for several years operated his own safari business there.

But Bigfoot was always in the back of his mind. Perhaps such an animal really lived in the forests of North America. If so, it would be one of the major remaining unsolved mysteries. In 1968 he was back in America.

This picture is described by the Bigfoot Information Center as "a composite picture of the Bigfoot based on many intimate descriptions." (*Photo:* © *Peter Byrne, The Bigfoot Information Center, The Dalles, Oregon*)

With the help of a few friends, he organized the International Wildlife Conservation Society, Inc., and in 1971 set out once more to track down Bigfoot.

Today the long search of Peter Byrne still goes on. His base is The Dalles, Oregon. His headquarters is the little museum where he answers questions for thousands of tourists.

This information center is also a convenient place for anyone to report any Bigfoot sighted. Byrne takes such reports seriously. As a result, the flow of information on Bigfoot continues. The Bigfoot Information Center publishes a newsletter, which is sent to interested subscribers anywhere.

Furthermore, there is a standing reward offered for good leads that might help Byrne and his associates learn more about this mysterious animal. All this. has brought fresh reports from a number of states, including several beyond those where Bigfoot is usually sighted. Arkansas has its large hairy apelike animal, and Florida had one reported briefly in the southern swamps.

Byrne knows better than most that some people like to play jokes on monster hunters. He calls these people "Piltdowners."

In his native England, in 1911, part of a human skull was dug from a gravel pit. When scientists saw that it had an apelike jaw, some believed it was from a human who had lived a million years ago. But scientists discovered eventually that the jaw of an ape had been

Peter Byrne, founder of the Bigfoot Information Center, The Dalles, Oregon, holds a plaster cast of a giant footprint believed to be that of a Bigfoot. (*Photo: International Harvester Company*)

attached to the human skull. The famous Piltdown Man, which had been taken so seriously, was a fake. Byrne takes great care to avoid being duped by the Piltdowners. Evidence left behind by the Piltdowners is easily detected by outdoorsmen of Byrne's experience in tracking.

Any new sighting of a Bigfoot can bring one of Byrne's co-workers hurrying to any part of the Northwest. They arrive with materials for making plaster casts, photographs, and sound recordings. Then they study the evidence to see if it adds new clues to the search for the forest monster.

An unusual story about Bigfoot comes from a missionary priest with whom Peter Byrne once talked. The priest spoke of an Indian he knew on Vancouver Island, in British Columbia, a rugged trapper named Muchalat Harry. He was known for his common sense and also for his fearlessness. Alone in the wilderness on an autumn night, Muchalat Harry wrapped himself in his blankets and lay down in his lean-to to sleep.

Later he awakened to find that he was being bundled in his blankets and tucked under the massive hairy arm of a giant male Bigfoot. The creature began moving off rapidly through the forest, carrying the helpless trapper.

Before daylight the Bigfoot stopped. Muchalat Harry found himself surrounded by Bigfoot creatures of various sizes, both male and female. Late that afternoon he slipped away from the Bigfoot camp and ran through the forest like the wind. He arrived back in his home village in the middle of the night, yelling for his friends to rescue him. He had run twelve miles and paddled his canoe another forty-five miles without slowing down. His shoes were gone and so were his outer clothes, everything but his underwear. The priest who told the story was among those who helped Muchalat Harry to his house. For several weeks the trapper crouched in his bed. His hair turned white. He recovered slowly. But never again did he leave the safety of his village, not even to return to the forest for his rifle and trapping equipment. Muchalat Harry wanted nothing more to do with Bigfoot, ever.

That was, as Peter Byrne recorded it, in 1928. Today the trail of Bigfoot still tempts the curious, but the mystery is no closer to being solved than it was then.

CHAPTER 10

The Missing Virginians

On summer evenings hundreds of people flock to a famous outdoor theater on the shore of North Carolina. With the sea breezes whispering through the live oaks and the gentle waves washing up on the shores of Roanoke Sound, they settle onto the benches beneath the stars. There they see again the old mystery unfold on the stage before them.

This drama, *The Lost Colony,* is a strange story that had its beginnings nearly four hundred years ago. England was building her first great ships. Her daring sea captains were being sent out to distant parts of the world to explore and claim land for England. The promise of new land lured them across the Atlantic to the wooded shores of North America.

On this stage at the Waterside Theater at the Fort Raleigh National Historic Site, actors re-create the drama of the colony that vanished. (*Photo: Aycock Brown*)

In 1578 the queen issued a charter to Sir Humphrey Gilbert. His instructions were to ". . . discover, search, find out, and view . . . remote heathen and barbarous lands . . . not actually possessed of any Christian prince and inhabited by Christian people." He was further authorized to take over such lands in the name of the queen and establish government over them.

But on his adventure to the wilderness shores of North America Sir Humphrey drowned. His half-brother, Walter Raleigh, wanted to continue the American adventure and carry on what his brother had started.

The following year the queen granted Walter Raleigh a charter and he outfitted two ships and dispatched them to North America.

Sir Walter's captains were jubilant with what they found in 1584. They sailed back to England to report on this "paradise of the world." The land they saw is today the coast of North Carolina. A journal written on the voyage told of "so sweet, and so strong a smell, as if we had been in the midst of some delicate garden abounding with all kinde of odoriferous flowers."

They told of vines loaded with sweet and juicy grapes growing wild for the picking. They added that the fishing was so productive that small boats could be filled to overflowing in scarcely any time at all.

In addition, they reported, as they had been told to do, on the nature of the people they found on these new shores, the red men. The Indians, they concluded, were "gentle, loving and faithful."

The queen was so pleased with the report that she promptly knighted Raleigh. The faraway land was named Virginia, in honor of the Virgin Queen. Raleigh began laying plans for a more ambitious invasion of the American coast, and preparations continued through the following winter.

By spring they were ready, and on April 9, 1585, a fleet of seven ships hoisted sail and eased out of the harbor at Plymouth, in southwestern England. The armada was under the command of Sir Richard Grenville, Sir Walter's cousin.

Seventy-five days later the ships deposited 108 men in a military mission on Roanoke Island, along the shore of North Carolina. They spent only one year in the new land. During that time they did some gardening but obtained much of their food from the Indians. Mostly, they were busy exploring this strange land. The exploring parties traveled 80 miles south along the coastal islands and bays, and 130 miles north. Meanwhile, the Indians they had thought peaceful watched and sometimes fought with these early white settlers.

The English pioneers built a fort on the north edge of Roanoke Island. Sometimes they stood on the shore watching the sea for ships on the horizon, because Sir Richard Grenville had returned to England for more supplies.

Meanwhile, Sir Francis Drake had been down in the Caribbean pursuing the Spanish. His ships, making their way back to England, detoured to check on the

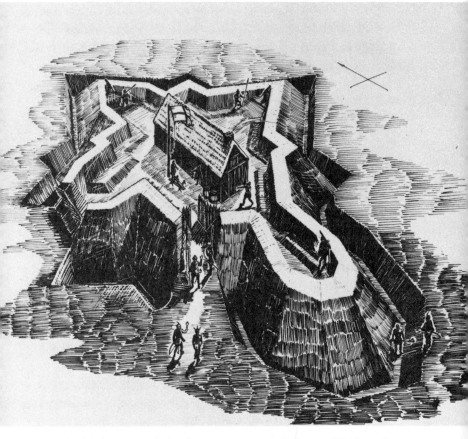

Fort Raleigh, scene of the famous mystery of the vanished settlers, is believed to have looked like this. (*Photo: National Park Service*)

colony at Roanoke Island. They found the men of Fort Raleigh eager to return to England with them. The Indians had not been friendly. Food was not always plentiful. Supplies were now gone, and nobody knew when more would come. The whole party left the fort on Drake's ships and turned across the Atlantic toward home.

Only two weeks later Sir Richard Grenville's ships arrived, loaded with new supplies. The fort stood empty and silent. Fifteen men were left behind to hold the queen's claims in Virginia.

Sir Walter Raleigh was still determined to carry out his plan to colonize America. What was needed was a group of permanent settlers, people who would clear the forests, build homes, raise children, and tame this wild and fruitful land.

His plans were made with great care. Among his settlers were to be skilled craftsmen and builders. Within the party of 121 people were 17 women and 9 children. Theirs was an exciting adventure into a new life. They were to become the first permanent English settlers in the New World.

They sailed in May 1587 aboard three ships, with John White as their governor. After seventy-six days at sea they reached the coast of North Carolina, where they expected to meet the fifteen men left to guard Fort Raleigh. But the men were gone without a trace, except for one, whose skeleton was found. Forcing thoughts of the lost men from their minds as best they

The entrance of the reconstructed Fort Raleigh on Roanoke Island,
North Carolina. (*Photo: National Park Service*)

could, and perhaps feeling some safety in numbers, the people set to work repairing the fort and the settlers' dwellings.

They also scoured the countryside nearby for wild foods, including fish and shellfish caught from the harbor. The third day after the group arrived, one of the men was wading in the shallow tidewaters of the bay, gathering clams for the evening meal. He had made a mistake in going out alone. Or perhaps his mistake was going out at all, because he was attacked by Indians and killed on the spot.

Other attacks by the Indians followed. Governor White kept a record of those early days of the colony. On August 18, 1587, he wrote that his daughter Eleanor, wife of Ananias Dare, had given birth to the first white child born in the New World. She was named Virginia. A few days later another child was born.

Meanwhile, leaders of the group checked the supplies and studied the chances that the colony could make it through the coming winter. They needed more salt, cattle, and other essentials for their permanent settlement. Governor White decided that he should personally return to England for these supplies and when his new granddaughter was only nine days old his ship put to sea. He left behind not only his daughter and granddaughter, but also his wife. He promised to return without delay.

At home, Governor White found his country threatened with invasion by the Spanish. There was no large ship he could obtain for the trip back across the Atlantic. He scouted around on his own until he found two small ships, then stocked them heavily with provisions for the American colony. He took aboard fifteen additional colonists.

They had gone only a short distance when a French ship stopped them, boarded, and stole all their supplies and property. So Governor White turned back to England.

There he learned that the situation with the Spanish had grown even worse. No longer could he use the two small ships. In the shadow of the Spanish threat he had to stay on in England month after month. Finally, in 1590, nearly three years after he had left his people on Roanoke, he sailed again for Virginia.

As they approached land they blew a trumpet to alert the colonists. But no one came running down the sandy shore to wave and welcome them. They went close to the shore in their small boats, climbed the sandy banks, and made their way toward the fort. But Governor White heard only the calls of the birds and the sounds of the waves dying on the beach. There was an unnatural silence over all the island. Not a single member of his party was any longer on the island. There was no sign of violence. The people were simply gone.

The lost colony of Roanoke became one of the great mysteries of American history. On a tree someone had

The church in which the lost colony worshiped is believed to have looked like this. (*Photo: National Park Service*)

carved the word *Croatan*. Perhaps the people had gone with the Croatan Indians, said to be a friendly tribe along the coast to the south. Even today some Indians of the coast speak of the white people who, long ago, were their ancestors. But early settlers who searched for whites among the Indian tribes never found them.

The mystery has never been solved and perhaps never will be. The lost colony of Roanoke remains lost. Only the outdoor drama at Fort Raleigh on summer evenings keeps the story fresh in our minds.

CHAPTER 11

Finding Water with a Stick

For hundreds of years farmers have dug wells, never knowing when they begin whether they will find water. But many are convinced that their chances are much better if they employ the services of a water witch.

The water witch uses a forked stick, usually from a willow, peach, or hazelnut tree, to indicate where water is located underground. One branch of the fork is gripped in each hand, and the point of the stick is held straight up. The water witch, who may also be called a "dowser," then begins walking over the area being tested, and if he crosses a water vein the point of the stick dips sharply toward the earth.

Furthermore, it bends with such force that there is precious little that the water witch can do to stop it.

Successful water dowsers tell of gripping the twig with all their power only to have either the bark twist off in their hands or the skin of their palms blistered by the moving stick.

Some dowsers use a wire from a coat hanger instead of a twig. Others use a pendulum and claim that it swings to show where water is.

Water dowsing has both its believers and its nonbelievers. Even those who believe in it are unable to explain why a stick should be influenced by water hidden in the earth.

No one can be certain how long men have used this technique for locating water and also minerals. There are records of its practice as far back as 1556 in Germany. During the 1600s witching for water was common in France. Then it spread all across Europe and later to America. There is no great difference between the methods used today and those employed hundreds of years ago. Sometimes the system works, sometimes it fails.

During the 1800s in England, John Mullins was greatly respected for his dowsing abilities—as well as for his honesty. One day Mullins was summoned by the owner of a large estate in the coal-mining country of Yorkshire. The coal mines tunneling beneath his property had drained all his wells.

The estate owner was not greatly impressed with Mullins at first. The water dowser said he was really a stone mason by profession. Through most of his life he had worked on a single estate. But he then discovered that he could find water with a forked stick and his life began to change. Mullins did not go through any spooky hokum or call up any magic powers with strange jungle words. Instead he simply went about his water-finding business as if it was one more chore for the day. For this he asked only a modest fee and his traveling expenses.

Many a water dowser would not dare wait around to see if the well diggers really found water where he had said it was. Some were fast-talk artists who swept through a neighborhood "finding" water, then were gone, never to be seen again. But not Mullins. He had faith. Once he had pinpointed the location of water, he did the actual digging himself.

Mullins worked through the fields above the hidden coal mines slowly until he was certain. He located springs the land owner had not known about before. When he finished, the estate owner had abundant water. Mullins left behind a whole neighborhood of farmers who had become strong believers in the art of water dowsing.

Even more famous was Evelyn Penrose, also of England. Miss Penrose had seen her father practice dowsing, then learned, while still young, that she too had the gift.

After finishing school, Miss Penrose traveled to California to visit an uncle. There her mysterious powers helped oil-well drillers find the best places for their wells. Next she traveled to Hawaii, where she located sources of water for sugar-plantation owners. In Canada, the British Columbia provincial government made her the official water-diviner to the government. She described this job in her book *Adventure Unlimited*. Her remarkable ability to locate water was responsible for taking her around the world with her magic wand.

"I felt strongly," she wrote, "that divining was not supernatural, or just a freak phenomenon, but was based on natural law; and I wanted, if possible, to discover what that law was and how it worked." When seeking water, Miss Penrose plunged through thickets, forgetting about rattlesnakes, briars, and thorns. "I am entirely unconscious of anybody or anything," she wrote, "apart from following the pull of the rod."

She claimed that she could locate water anywhere in the world from a map without visiting the area. Another who was said to possess this skill was a famous American dowser, Henry Gross, of Maine.

He first began to understand the value of his gift while still in school in New Hampshire. An elderly friend demonstrated for Henry one day the way hidden water veins make a forked stick bend downward. Henry promptly took the stick and found that he, too, had the power to find water in this wonderful manner.

His first test came when he was twelve. The school he attended was in serious need of a new well. Nobody knew where it would be best to dig, and at this point Henry said he would be glad to find the best place in the schoolyard for the well. He began walking around the schoolyard with his forked stick. At last it bent down strongly. The well diggers were down only six or seven feet when they suddenly had water over their boot tops. Henry Gross was very important that day in his school. This was the beginning of his remarkable career in water witching.

After he grew up Henry Gross became a game warden in Maine. But he was never so busy protecting deer, rabbits, and grouse that he could not stop long enough to find the best location for a farmer's well. So sensitive was Gross's body to underground water that he once had to move his bed to another part of the room; the bed had been placed above a water vein and the presence of that hidden water directly below him disturbed his sleep.

He could even talk to his peach stick and it would tell him how much water was flowing in a vein. Historical novelist Kenneth Roberts, a friend of Gross, told about this in his book *Henry Gross and His Dowsing Rod*. Gross held his divining rod above the hidden water vein and asked it questions. If it dipped downward after a question, Gross took it as a "yes" answer. By this system, he determined that the vein beneath his bedroom flowed at a rate of three to four quarts per minute. Now Gross could not only locate water for farmers, but could tell them how strong the flow would be. He said he could even trust the rod to tell him if the water was polluted.

His most remarkable accomplishment, however, was in locating supplies of abundant underground water on the island of Bermuda. He knew nothing about the island and had never been there. He used his dowsing rod over a map of the island, eight hundred miles away. The new wells he located were found, according to Roberts, just in time to save Bermuda from a serious drought.

Most scientists still doubt that anyone has these strange powers. Water witching is difficult to explain. Those who do try to explain the mystery speak of forces passing from the water through the rod to the person holding it. Miss Penrose believed that water, minerals, and oil give off "electromagnetic waves and fields of force." The water dowser is said to become a receiving set, picking up messages transmitted by the hidden water. The argument continues. On the one side are the scientists insisting that water witching can amount to little because there is no scientific way to explain it. On the other side are the believers insisting that water witching works whether we understand it or not.

Some years ago two professors, Evon Z. Vogt and Ray Hyman, sent questionnaires to hundreds of county agricultural extension agents around the country. They asked questions about the water witches operating in those counties, and how successful they were. This study convinced the professors that water witching does not work. They admitted that water witches sometimes

find water, but agreed that water witching is not relia-
ble, and is founded on superstition and a belief in
magic.

All my scientific training tells me that they must be
right. But as I concluded my writing on this chapter I
laid the work aside and went out into the open field
beyond our old farmhouse. I was curious. I located a
peach tree and cut a forked stick that looked like those
I have seen water witches use.

With the stick in my hands, I began walking back
and forth slowly across the field. At first nothing happened. Then the stick seemed to be tipping toward the
ground.

I don't know what's down there. I don't know what
made the stick bend. I believe there was no motion of
the muscles in my hands that would have turned it, but
I cannot be certain of that. All I know is that the stick
turned down. This much was observable. Beyond that
lies the mystery.

CHAPTER 12

Mysteries of a Jungle Civilization

One morning some years ago, I stopped at the desk in my hotel in Belize City to ask about visiting ruins of the mysterious Mayan civilization. These people built cities and magnificent stone temples where they sometimes offered human sacrifices to their gods. Ruins of these cities have been found deep in the jungles of Mexico and Central and South America, and today the story of their remarkable civilization has never been fully explained.

I was told about an excavation some miles out of the city where a group of archaeologists from an American university was working. A few minutes later our rattling old taxicab was carrying us out of town and toward the jungle.

We bounced over chuckholes and rocks as we followed twisting narrow trails that wound through the forests. There was an occasional opening where a farmer had built his house and cleared enough land to grow his vegetables.

After traveling for nearly an hour the taxicab suddenly broke free of the jungle. We eased out into a broad sunny clearing. An ancient temple stood at one side of the opening where the blankets of vines and trees had been cut away. Nearby were thatched shelters used by the scientists when they were not busy studying the giant stone temple.

The ancestors of the Maya came originally from Asia. When much of the earth's moisture was frozen in giant glaciers, the oceans held less water than they do today. As sea level fell lower and lower, a broad bridge of land rose through the surface of the Pacific between Asia and North America. Over this bridge between the continents, living creatures of many kinds moved. They crossed in both directions. Many doubtless were following their sources of food. Along with the animals moving toward the New World came the Stone Age people who hunted them, the ancestors of the Indians, Aleuts, and Eskimos. Eventually these tribes spread over the continent and southward into Central and South America.

Only the Maya Indians developed their own complex written language. Some of them became skilled astronomers. They worked out a calendar similar to the one

Ancient Mayan artists created splendid temples and carvings. This is a scene at Chichén Itzá, Yucatán, in Mexico. (*Photo: Mexican National Tourist Council*)

we use today, basing their work on observations of the stars. They also created a system of mathematics and this helped them design their complicated buildings.

This civilization was at its peak from about 250 to 900 A.D. Five hundred years before Columbus arrived in the islands of the Caribbean the Mayan civilization was already disappearing. How the Mayan people built their advanced civilization and why it then vanished became one of the world's great mysteries.

Ruins of their great cities are scattered through the jungles of Mexico and Central America. They lived in Mexico, especially in the Yucatán Peninsula, and in Guatemala, Belize, and Honduras.

Mayan farmers and their families lived in huts made with walls of poles and roofs of thatched grass and palm leaves. But others lived in gleaming cities with stone buildings and giant temples. Such cities, and the countryside surrounding them, are called "city-states" by modern scientists studying the Mayan culture. There were numerous city-states throughout the jungles, and each had its own high priests and scholars.

The Maya worshiped many gods, the god of the sun, the god of corn, and the gods of rain who blessed the plantings. Their stone temples were the centers of religious ceremonies. Humans sacrificed to the gods were sometimes captured in warfare among the Mayan people. Wars may have been a part of their religious activities.

The Maya played a form of basketball on courts located in the temples. The game was deadly serious. A hard rubber ball was bounced against the wall and players tried to put it through a hoop. But, unlike modern basketball players, they could not use their hands. Instead, they could bounce the ball with only their hips or knees. This ancient game had another important difference from modern basketball: the losing team might be led to the high altars on top of the temple and there be sacrificed in sacred religious ceremonies.

Chichén Itzá, a Mayan site in Yucatán, has two giant wells that puzzled investigators for many years. One was for water supply, but the other was believed to have been part of the religious ceremonies. Each well was about 65 feet deep and from 165 to 200 feet in diameter, with as much as 40 feet of water standing in the bottom.

Recently archaeologists brought up jewelry from the bottom of one of these wells. There were bracelets, rings, necklaces, earrings, and pendants of gold, copper, and jade, as well as beautiful ornaments made of shells. From these finds and other studies, the story has been gradually unraveled. In times of drought this well, like the altars of the temples, became a place for human sacrifice.

If the tropical sun beat down upon the hard brown fields and the crops withered and died, the priests knew that Chac, the rain god, was not pleased. There must be sacrifices to appease the god. Those selected for sacrifice were young people. Draped with precious or-

The Temple of the Warriors at Chichén Itzá. (*Photo: Mexican National Tourist Council*)

naments, the victims were led to the edge of the great well. There they were thrown into the well to drown.

These are bits of the puzzling story of the Maya. Scientists have unraveled part of the story by studying hieroglyphics and sculptures found in their temples.

As builders, the Maya Indians were superb. They cut and moved massive blocks of stone. They learned how to make concrete and how to plaster their temples to smooth the rough edges where the stones met. The walls of rooms where the priests lived were plastered. The temples rose seventy-five feet and more above the jungle floor and long flights of broad stone steps led to the top. A strange feeling settled over us as we climbed those stairs used a thousand years ago.

The building was done with many tools. But there were no metal tools with which to shape the stones. The Mayan people did not even have the wheel to help them move heavy burdens. Neither did they have horses or other domestic beasts to help them lift the huge stones into place.

Roads surfaced with stone connected the cities. People walked these highways carrying goods from their farms to markets in the cities.

In addition to walking, these people used canoes for transportation on the rivers.

Most of the Mayan people were farmers. They used sticks to dig the earth, and planted squash, beans, corn, sweet potatoes, cotton, tobacco, and cacao. They cleared the jungle, usually with fire, grew their crops,

Sculpture on a temple at the famous Mayan site of Palenque, in Mexico. (*Photo: Mexican National Tourist Council*)

and when the richness of the soil was gone, they moved and opened new fields.

But it was not the tilling of the soil that set the Mayan Indians apart from others. Agriculture was widely practiced by other people. The Mayan farmers, however, had food abundant enough to provide for other classes that did not have to grow their own food. The priests could spend their time studying astronomy and mathematics. Merchants could buy and sell. Laborers could build great temples. Painters and sculptors were freed of farming to create their works of art.

Then, one by one the city-states, once busy with the coming and going of hundreds of people, grew quieter and were abandoned.

What happened to the Mayan civilization? Even scientists who have studied the structures and the writings of these Indians can only guess at the cause of their downfall. Today there are a million and a half Maya Indians still living in Central America. But these people remember no legends that might explain what happened to their ancestors, who were farmers, scientists, and scholars.

Some believe that the peasants may have overthrown the priests in open rebellion. But what seems more likely is that the population grew beyond the ability of the fields to feed the people, and hunger conquered the civilization.

When the Spanish arrived in the 1500s the temples were already being reclaimed by the jungle. The

Explorations have uncovered some of the mysteries of the Mayan people. (*Photo: Mexican National Tourist Council*)

Spanish conquerors destroyed much of what was left. Until then perhaps the story of the Mayan people was preserved in the fragile books that the priests had written on bark cloth, stories that would have solved mysteries for modern scholars. But the Spanish soldiers were ordered to find and burn these books as the devil's work. All but three were lost.

Temples left to the jungle are soon covered with vines and trees. Roots pry old stones apart. Time and weather chip the plaster away. Skilled hands and trained scientists can restore the ancient temples, and although the evidence is assembled a bit at a time, the rise and fall of Mayan civilization is still a deep and puzzling mystery.

CHAPTER 13

ESP—the Inner Mystery

Most scientists work with facts. They deal with what they can see, measure, take apart, or put together. Everything falls into place. There is a neatness and a sense of order to such research. The result is satisfying because it is real and it clears up another mystery.

But there is another kind of research, one that explores the supernatural. Some scientists spend their time studying ghostly happenings. They want to understand why special people receive messages they cannot see, hear, feel, smell, or taste. Instead of these standard five senses that all of us have and all of us know, there may be, say these scientists of the supernatural, extra senses that carry messages if only we can recognize them. Some people, they say, may have ESP, extrasensory perception. Those who possess this mysterious mental telepathy sometimes baffle all of us with their remarkable observations.

They may receive messages from faraway places, messages flashed from one mind to another. They may forecast the future, heal the sick, or solve crimes by calling on mysterious powers.

Such evidence of the supernatural has fascinated people for centuries, and today the interest in ESP is greater than ever. In one survey of English scientists and technicians, 67 per cent said that they considered ESP a fact or a definite possibility. Scientists studying ESP can be found working in the laboratories of universities in the United States, Canada, Russia, and elsewhere around the world. They have a special name for their science, parapsychology. They probe the secret world of the unknown, the hidden depths of the mind.

Some scientists dismiss the parapsychologists as freaks. They accuse them of wasting time, money, and energy trying to prove that the unreal is real. Others insist that all scientists should have freedom to explore the unknown. One thing is certain: the parapsychologists have uncovered many mysterious cases and puzzling examples.

For three years recently scientists at the Electronics and Bioengineering Laboratory of the Stanford Research Institute in California studied what they call "remote viewing." These investigators found that human subjects could sit in the laboratory and describe what people were doing thousands of miles away.

One of these scientists took a trip to Costa Rica, four thousand kilometers from his laboratory in California. Another scientist working with him in the laboratory brought in people who had never been to Costa Rica. These people were asked to describe what the scientist was doing in Costa Rica at the moment. When the traveling scientist returned, he carried back a written record of his daily activities in Costa Rica. The accuracy of the remote viewing back in the laboratory was amazing.

One subject sitting in the laboratory was surprised at the images he received from Costa Rica. Instead of the mountains of Costa Rica he had the definite impression that the scientist was at an airport near a sandy beach. There was a small building and this was also described.

The scientist back in California in the laboratory could not understand this. He knew his fellow scientist's plans and nothing in the plans called for airplane travel off the island. But what he did not know was that the traveler had taken an unplanned one-day side trip by plane to a nearby island. The air strip described in the laboratory matched the description given by the traveling scientist, including the sand and the small building. In addition, the remote-viewing session occurred at the exact time the scientist in Costa Rica was landing more than two thousand miles away.

Similar experiments conducted more than fifty times have shown the Stanford scientists that many people can learn to use this ability for remote viewing of subjects whether in the next room or far away.

Among the people most famous for the gift was Edgar Cayce of Kentucky. Cayce was not a doctor. He was not even well educated. Newspaper stories of his day referred to him as illiterate.

But Cayce could go into a trance, and when he spoke, words he had never heard came from his mouth. Doctors hearing him were amazed at the medical terms he used, at the diagnoses he made, and the treatments he prescribed while in a trance. They were also astounded at the cures he was able to bring to hundreds of afflicted people.

Cayce always insisted that he had no control over this gift. There was, he said, a force outside himself that put the strange words into his mouth. He was only the instrument, a receiver of messages.

His psychic readings became famous beginning in 1901. They continued, hundreds of them, until Cayce died in 1945.

By trade Cayce was a clerk in a small store. He was a quiet man and deeply religious. He refused to use his gift of ESP to make money. Instead, he considered it his responsibility to help people with his power. He was convinced that if he misused it for his own gain he would lose the gift and then be unable to help anyone.

Among his earliest cases was that of little Amy Detrich. Amy was the daughter of the local school superintendent in Hopkinsville, Kentucky, where Cayce lived. When she was two years old she became ill. By the age of five Amy was considered a hopeless cripple. Local doctors predicted that she would soon die. Specialists in large city clinics examined her and agreed that they could do nothing.

Then as a last resort her parents turned to an osteopath, the only medical man in Hopkinsville who had not tried to help the child. The osteopath called in a young friend of his, Edgar Cayce.

Cayce lay down upon a couch. He relaxed, then passed into one of his trances. He did not know Amy Detrich or anything about her. But while he was in a trance he was told about the doomed child and her medical history. Next he was asked to describe Amy's problem. He spoke in strong, clear tones. From the mouth of Edgar Cayce came jawbreaker medical terms. He explained what treatment must be given. This treatment was carried out. Within a few weeks she had completely recovered and afterward lived the life of a normal little girl.

Cayce found that he could help people even if he never saw them. All that was needed was for him to be in a trance and be told to think about a certain person's ailment. Then, as if his mind were a medical computer filled with modern scientific facts, he would begin to speak. Afterward, when he was awake again, Cayce could not remember what he had said in the trance. This did not disturb him or even appear unusual to him. Why should it? He always insisted that when in a trance he was not the one doing the talking.

One medical doctor who worked with Cayce reported to a convention of physicians that Cayce had helped him with about one hundred cases. This physician, a highly respected man in Hopkinsville, had never known Cayce to make an error in diagnosis.

His psychic ability went beyond helping the sick. In one case an elderly woman had been shot and killed in a city five hundred miles from his home. Police could make no progress on the puzzling case. They had no idea who had committed the crime, what motive there might have been, or where the gun was.

Then a traveling man passing through Hopkinsville talked of the crime with Cayce's father. The elder Cayce said his son could pinpoint the murderer. He put Edgar into a trance, and after some time the answers began to come. The gun, Cayce said, was a Colt .45. One shot had been fired. The gun had been thrown out a window. It was, at that moment, lying in the edge of a drainpipe. Furthermore, the crime had been committed by the elderly lady's sister.

The police were told of Cayce's message. They went to the roof of the building and, moving along carefully, came to the drainpipe Cayce had mentioned. Looking down into the corner of the pipe, they saw the gun exactly where they had been told to look.

Next, a detective arrived in Hopkinsville to arrest Cayce. Nobody but the murderer, they said, could possibly have known about the gun. There was one thing wrong with this conclusion: Cayce had not been out of his home town for the past eight years. Besides, at about that time, the victim's sister confessed that it was she who had fired the fatal shot. Cayce had known neither of the sisters nor had any clues to guide him. But the facts of the case had come through his mind as if this were a mystery story he himself had written. Again, as he awakened from his trance he could recall nothing he had said.

By the time Edgar Cayce died in Virginia Beach, Virginia, he had founded his Association for Research and Enlightenment. Here, even after his death, studies would continue of the mysterious cases and of all the people he had helped during his remarkable lifetime. He left files on more than fourteen thousand such readings. There have been countless magazine and newspaper articles and many books about Edgar Cayce. But no one has yet explained his mysterious power.

Some people practice a brand of healing known in the eastern mountains as the laying on of hands. An elderly friend of mine once told me of seeing his father perform such healings. He said he did not understand how it happened. All he knew was that his father had a special power in his hands.

There seems no reason to believe that my friend made up his stories. He was apparently only recalling things from his childhood as he remembered them.

He remembered the day his little sister spilled scalding water down her arm. The child screamed with pain, and the arm turned red and began to blister. Her father hurried from the barn. In the kitchen he held the little girl's arm up and ran his other hand along the full length of the burned flesh.

The crying stopped. The pain was gone. The burned arm was no longer sore and the redness had vanished.

Another time my friend was bringing in a team of mules from the hay field. He was then about thirteen, and he recalls that day vividly. "When I was opening the gate," he told me, "the mules became tangled in the barbed wire on the gate. One of them fell down and began kicking and rolling in the wire. There was nothing I could do. When the mule finally got up, a whole sheet of its hide had been torn loose and was hanging down like a flap against its leg. I never saw anything bleed the way that mule was bleeding."

He took the frightened team to the barn. There, his father took one look at the valuable animal and its serious injury. "He just ran the palm of his hand over the torn place," my friend recalled, "and the bleeding stopped. It healed up in a few days and the mule was as good as ever."

Some would say suggestion helps a psychic heal with his hands. Perhaps a little girl seeing her father perform an act that is supposed to heal her gets well faster because she actually believes she will improve. But it is doubtful that the power of suggestion ever worked on a mule.

CHAPTER 14

Animals and ESP

There is no reason to believe that humans are the only animals capable of receiving messages through other than the normal senses. We may never succeed in explaining these strange forces, but we cannot ignore the facts. At least some lower animals display powerful evidence of ESP.

What else could account for the travels of Fluke's Maltese cat? My friend Richard Fluke told me the story. "My father had a cat that was the best mouser I ever saw. He was famous around the neighborhood for keeping the mice under control.

"My father worked on the railroad and his route took him from Cincinnati across Ohio to Pennsylvania. He had this friend there who said the mice were about to take over his home and farm, and my father said he had the answer to that. He promised to bring his cat up on his next run and let him keep the cat until the mice were cleaned out."

Fluke, dressed in his railroading clothes and carrying his lunch pail, gathered up the cat and set off for work. The train made its way up across Ohio. It traveled more than two hundred miles.

Eventually the train reached Steubenville, on the Ohio border. It slowed down, and as it did, Fluke's cat leaped through an open window. There was nothing Mr. Fluke could do. The train sped on, and the cat was left behind in strange country it had never seen before.

"We all thought we would never see the cat again," Richard Fluke told me. "But thirteen days later that cat was back home scratching on the door to be let in. Its feet were raw and bloody from traveling. Now you tell me how that cat knew its way home over more than two hundred miles of strange country!"

Where animals follow regular migration routes there are explanations for their ability to navigate. The migrating birds follow routes used by their ancestors. Their migration patterns are believed to be genetically fixed and so much a part of each bird that the bird must obey the regular impulses to migrate. Scientists believe they may be guided by sunlight, stars, magnetic fields, or combinations of these. All of these forces and influences can be explained in rather exact scientific terms.

But these are regular migrations along routes known to each species of bird for thousands of years. The ability of an animal to find its way home calls for something additional. Homing pigeons are the most famous animals for locating their home again from wherever they are released. Numerous other animals, including Mr. Fluke's cat, also possess this strange sense.

Dog owners often tell stories of astounding trips their animals have made from distant places. Among the more remarkable stories I have heard was that of a foxhound named Hightail.

This hound's unforgettable adventure was described to me by George Jett, an Illinois farmer. Hightail grew up on the farm of Harley Burch, who was Jett's friend. Burch lived 120 miles from Jett's place and he kept and trained the dog for her real owner.

Hightail developed a reputation early in life as a superior foxhound. Her pups were much in demand. Eventually Hightail's owner died, and H. L. Cooper, a Baptist minister who was a very serious fox hunter, arranged to take old Hightail over to his place in Virginia. She was getting old but he thought she might still raise a couple of litters of pups to carry on her fine bloodlines. Burch sadly crated her up and shipped her off to Virginia.

During the next two years Hightail raised two litters of pups. But she was growing old and no longer had the stout muscles and strong reflexes that had once carried her over the trails and through the long nights.

These dogs, similar to Hightail, may possess strange extrasensory powers that account for their remarkable homing abilities. Similar abilities are possessed by many animals, wild and domestic. (*Photo: George Laycock*)

Then one day an automobile struck her and after that she limped, was deaf in both ears, and could see with only one eye.

When she was thirteen, George Jett, thinking Hightail might still bear one more litter of pups, asked Rev. H. L. Cooper to send her out to his farm in Illinois. He met the old dog at the railroad station and took her back to the farm, where she had never been before.

"I took one look at her," Jett told me, "and said, 'Old girl, you're not going anyplace,' and I gave her the run of the farm."

But some strange longing worked within old Hightail. She was approaching death, but she was now within 120 miles of where she and Harley Burch had hunted together in her youth. When Jett went looking for the old hound that evening, she was gone.

One night two weeks later, Harley Burch was sitting on a hillside listening to his foxhounds on a trail. Then a strange dog limped slowly into the edge of the light cast by his fire. To Burch the hound looked like a ghost. He examined her collar. Then he put his arms around the old hound and a tear edged down his cheek. Later he called Jett and told him what had happened. With a break in his voice he said he would send Hightail back if Jett wanted him to. "No, you keep her," Jett said, "if she wanted that much to come back home, that's where she belongs."

Many pets apparently know when it is time for their masters to return home each day. Their biological clocks are set. An animal's senses become attuned to regular events that happen day after day. Then, as the time approaches, the animal anticipates the event. It may be feeding time. It may be the return of the master. It may be other events that "tell" the animal what is about to happen.

But this would not explain the strange story of the dog once owned by another friend. During the day when its mistress was at work the dog would do nothing but wait for her to return. The dog always knew twenty minutes ahead of time when she was coming. But she came home at different times every day. No matter what time she arrived, the dog had gone to the door and scratched twenty minutes earlier. Eventually its owners understood that the driving time home from where the lady worked was twenty minutes. In some mysterious way the dog knew when she left work and was on her way home.

Pet owners do not know how animals accomplish these remarkable feats. Neither do scientists. But the parapsychologists, carrying out research on ESP, may someday tell us what it is beyond the usual known senses that gives special messages to these animals.

CHAPTER 15

Island of the Forgotten

For the people of the island, the years came and went without change. The world beyond their shores was unknown to them. Their land lay in the warm bright sun of the Pacific. There, year after year, they fished the clean waters, raised their crops, and conducted their mysterious ceremonies out of sight of the rest of the world.

Then one spring day a vessel with huge white sails appeared on the horizon. The islanders stopped their work to stare in wonder. Slowly the ship edged closer to the island.

The people saw the men on the ships. They watched them lowering the longboats. Lines of sailors climbed down into the boats. The islanders rushed down to the shores to be there when the strangers arrived.

Standing in the first longboat was Jacob Roggeveen. The Dutch captain was puzzled by this island. It was not supposed to be where he had discovered it. There was no such island on any of the maps used by navigators. This was Easter Day, 1722, so Roggeveen called the place Easter Island.

The men in the longboats carried firearms because they were suspicious of native people. In the confusion of the meeting, with curious islanders rushing down to the shore, someone raised his gun. There was a shot and one of the natives fell to the ground. Other sailors followed the example. Soon a dozen of the islanders lay dead on the beach.

This was only the beginning of a long list of troubles brought to the people of Easter Island by outsiders. In later years visitors introduced diseases that took the lives of hundreds. Ships hauled the people away into slavery. Gradually the number of natives fell, until by 1934 there were no more than 175 remaining on the 64-square-mile island.

But murder and vandalism alone would never have made this island famous. Since prehistoric times, other invaders in other places have killed people and destroyed their temples and villages. The island, however, became famous because of great mysterious stone statues Roggeveen found on his first visit. The unbelievable carvings stood side by side along the seashore on long sloping stone platforms. The people came there to conduct religious ceremonies.

Over the years, as other ships stopped at Easter Island, many of the statues were toppled from their bases and broken. But others remained, some beside the sea, some inland. Some were simply too big to destroy easily. A century ago, when scientists first began to study the statues, there were perhaps a hundred of them remaining. They ranged in size from giants standing thirty-six feet above their bases to small ones three feet high. The large ones have been estimated to weigh as much as eighty tons. All of them were carved by stone tools, and moved and set in position by people who had no wheels, no beasts of burden, nor any modern aids to help them. Even today, given the roughness of Easter Island, such a task would be a major engineering operation.

Scientists discovered where the statues had been made. At the northeast end of the island, in the crater of an ancient volcano, was a large quarry. There the ancient sculptors had chipped and cut at the soft volcanic stone. Modern scholars estimate that the carving of just one of the statues might have taken twenty sculptors a year or more.

Eventually, however, the statue would take shape, and when completed it would look like all the others. Each of the statues on Easter Island is of a large human head and upper part of the body. The long, gaunt stone face turns slightly upward. The ears are

On Easter Island, huge stone statues, all alike except for size, stand with backs to the sea as they have for hundreds of years. Why they were carved or how they were moved is part of the mystery of Easter Island. (*Lan-Chile Airlines*)

large. Originally each of the statues was fitted with a huge stone crown, made separately and lifted into place on the finished carving.

The sculptors may have been still at work when Easter Island was first visited by European people. Later scientists who saw the quarry found carvings abandoned in various stages of completion. Around them were many of the tools that had been used in creating them. The craftsmen had stood on little shelves around the rock, chipping away with their stone chisels until the statue took on its form.

No one has ever discovered how these huge statues were moved from the quarry to the seashore. Some primitive people moved large stones by pulling them with ropes and rolling them on other round stones. But could an eighty-ton statue have been moved in such a way? A road once reached for six miles over rough terrain from the quarry to the seashore where most of the statues stood. Once a statue was at the shore, it still had to be inched up the incline and onto its platform, where it was placed facing inward toward the heart of Easter Island.

No one knows how long the ancient people occupied this island, but some of the statues are so weathered that they are believed to have been there for many centuries. Native people living there now are believed to be the descendants of those who fashioned the statues. Those people also had their own written language, examples of which have been found on wooden engravings discovered on Easter Island.

Almost certainly the statues played a central role in religious ceremonies. Roggeveen reported very little about the native customs. The islanders no longer remember the ceremonies, legends, or social organization of their ancestors.

We know they built houses of poles set in holes in the rocks. Bits of evidence tell us that these homes were long narrow buildings. People of the island also lived in caves.

Today Easter Island is ruled by a South American country, Chile, twenty-three hundred miles to the east. The ancient people who lived on Easter Island were separated from all other people by hundreds of miles in all directions. The nearest inhabited island, Pitcairn, is a thousand miles away.

So this is an island steeped in mystery, with far more questions than answers. Time has swallowed the evidence that might have solved the riddles. Above all there remains the mystery of the giant stone faces, dozens of them, standing silent guard over this remote Pacific island. Why were they carved? How were they moved? Exactly what did they mean to the people of Easter Island?

This is only one more of the world's great unanswered questions, another of the mysteries to which we may never know the full answer.

INDEX

GEORGE LAYCOCK has written more than thirty books on natural history and conservation. He has also written several hundred articles for many national magazines, including AUDUBON, NATIONAL WILDLIFE, FIELD AND STREAM, SPORTS ILLUSTRATED, REDBOOK, READER'S DIGEST, BETTER HOMES AND GARDENS, and BOY'S LIFE. When he writes of animals and the outdoors, he deals with subjects of lifelong interest. He is a native of Ohio, and holds a degree in wildlife management from the Ohio State University. He has traveled and camped widely, gathering information and making pictures for his articles and books.